# The Doctrine of The Lesser Magistrates

A Proper Resistance to Tyranny and a Repudiation of Unlimited Obedience to Civil Government



Matthew Trewhella

ISBN: 1482327686

ISBN 13: 9781482327687

Library of Congress Control Number: 2013902222
CreateSpace Independent Publishing Platform
North Charleston, South Carolina

# On the Cover

The nobles at Runnymede demonstrating the doctrine of
the lesser magistrates by interposing against the tyranny of King John in 1215 AD. The signing of the Magna Carta.

Cover sketch by Nicole Charpentier.

*For Christ,*
*Who set me free.*

*(Galatians 5:1; First Peter 2:16)*

# TABLE OF CONTENTS

# ACKNOWLEDGMENTS

Though countless people have influenced my life and worldview, there are a few that I must thank for being instrumental in helping make this book a concrete reality. First, I would like to thank Paul and Sue Lagan for the use of their cabin on the Mississippi River, a true oasis for thought, and getting the pen onto the paper. I also want to thank Cathy Ramey, Dr. Patrick Johnston, Paul Korzenko, and Rev. Forsell Gappa for their help with syntax, as well as inspiring much thought as the work progressed. Thank you also to Kent Hovind, who, while in bonds, encouraged me to write further on this topic.

I also want to thank my wife, Clara, whose love and encouragement for over three decades of marital union has made me a much better man. Rarely in life, so it seems these days, do two people taste the depths of the Lord's wisdom in establishing the institution of marriage. We taste it! The foundation of our union as husband and wife was sealed in Christ. The mortar of our union is our love and fealty for Him, and our undying love for one another. The fruit of our union is our children, and our children's children. Words fail in expressing my love for her. If not for her, this book would not be in your hands right now.

Finally, I would like to thank and honor those lesser magistrates who in years gone by have stood against tyranny, hazarding their lives in obedience and love for God, or simply their desire to do right. And to all those yet to come, may He give you wisdom and strength, and may you do right by Him.

# INTRODUCTION

In the course of human history, the abuse of authority by men through the arm of the State is not an uncommon occurrence. Western Civilization has pillared safeguards to help prevent this. Nevertheless, a citizenry must remain vigilant, and understand both the purpose and limitations of the State.

If a citizenry does not know the purpose and limitations of the State, then the civil government can misuse its power because the citizenry is unable to measure when something improper is occurring. For there to be any indignation towards acts of tyranny by the State, one must be able to recognize that tyranny is taking place.

Aldous Huxley, in his book, *Brave New World*, wrote of a citizenry of slaves who would love their enslavement. Huxley writes:

> A really efficient totalitarian state would be one in which the all-powerful executive of political bosses and their army of managers control a population of slaves *who do not have to be coerced, because they love their servitude.*[1]

Unknowingly, Americans have accepted the role of Huxley's servant-minded people for decades. This is due in part to the fact that people love comfort and tend to avoid conflict. However, the other part of the equation is that people have lost the yardstick by which they should measure the limits of government. As a consequence, we in America have become a slave-like people with the Federal government acting more as a Master, than as a Servant providing justice for the people.

1 Aldous Huxley, *Brave New World* (Garden City, NY: International Collectors Library, 1946) Foreword xiii.

When you go to Washington, D.C. today you cannot help but notice that it has become like a fortress. The heavily fortified nature of the place reminds one of what Plato said to the tyrant Dionysius when he saw him on the streets of Sicily surrounded by his many bodyguards – *"What harm have you done that you should need to have so many guards?"*[2]

In a very real sense, one is right to say our Federal government has harmed the American people. Review the current Federal laws, policies, and bureaucracies, and you cannot help but see that it has caused *much harm* to the institutions and traditions of our people. It is as if, over the course of time, we have been attacked and plundered.

In the past, the pulpits in our nation instructed the people in the purpose, functions, and limitations of the State. Many pastors preached every year what became known as "election" and "artillery" sermons. These sermons were routinely preached during the first 100 years of our nation. Clergymen understood and taught their congregations that God's Word addressed all matters of life, including the matters of civil government.

Today however, most pulpits are silent about God's Word when it comes to civil government. In fact, most just teach unlimited obedience to the State, as though there are no limitations to the State's rule. By default, they teach that whatever the civil government rules legislatively is therefore the will of God.

This type of clergymen was even present near the Revolutionary War era. The Rev. William Gordon of Roxbury, Massachusetts preached regarding such men in 1794 when he declared:

> Though the partisans of arbitrary power will freely censure that preacher who speaks boldly for the liberties of the people, they will admire as an excellent divine, the parson whose discourse is wholly in the opposite, *and teaches, that magistrates have a divine right for doing wrong, and are to be implicitly obeyed;* men professing Christianity, as if the religion of the blessed Jesus bound them to bow their neck to any tyrant.[3]

---

2 John of Salisbury, *The Statesman's Book of John of Salisbury – Policraticus,* trans. John Dickinson (New York, NY: Russell & Russell, 1159/1963) 17.

3 William Gordon, *The History of the Rise, Progress and Establishment of the United States of America, including An Account of the Late War,* 3 vols., 2d ed. (New York, 1794), I, 273–74.

The authority of the State does have limits. America's present day pulpits need to repent of their idolatrous views regarding the State. True Christianity produces liberty. Even the Christ-hating, 17th century philosopher, David Hume, had to admit:

> The precious sparks of liberty were kindled and preserved by the Puritans in England. And that, to this sect, whose principles appear so frivolous and whose habits so ridiculous, *the English owe the whole freedom of their Constitution.*[4]

The church pulpits are the historical means whereby the people are instructed, from a theological foundation, in the purpose, functions, and limitations of the State. When a citizenry's view of the State is theologically-driven, the State can no longer get away with doing whatever just tickles its fancy. This is because an informed citizenry, one which recognizes transcendent law, is vigilant, and will not tolerate abuse or tyranny.

First Corinthians 7:23 commands, *"Do not become the slaves of men."* Because of human nature, however, men tend to want to be ruled and "cared for," rather than take on responsibility and cherish liberty. Because of human nature, tyranny from time to time raises its ugly head. Because of human nature, men will endure a long train of abuses and usurpations.

However, men will endure a long train of abuses and usurpations – *only to a certain point.* When the civil government continues to assault men's rights and liberties through unconstitutional, unjust or immoral laws, policies, or bureaucratic decrees, honorable men will eventually weary of it, and begin to take a stand. Those men who do begin to stand, however, want to be assured that their efforts are legitimate and proper.

Thankfully, America's founders established three well-known "boxes" by which we can preserve liberty and resist tyranny. They are - the ballot box, the jury box, and the cartridge box.

The ballot box provides opportunity to remove unjust rulers through the vote.

The jury box provides citizens not only the right to judge the facts in a case, but to judge the law itself. The jury can determine whether a law is being misapplied or can find a law unjust or immoral altogether.

4 David Hume, *The History of England* (New York, NY: Harper & Brothers Publishers, 1688/1851) 141.

The jury can acquit on either basis, regardless of what the judge or jury instructions say.

The cartridge box refers to an armed citizenry. America's Founders knew that an armed citizenry not only helps repel an invading foreign force, but also acts as a check against tyranny from our own government.

But a lesser-known tool which the founders themselves employed is *the doctrine of the lesser magistrates.* The lesser magistrate doctrine provides the best means to rein in a higher authority that has spurned its limitations. The doctrine of the lesser magistrates is rooted in Scripture and found throughout the history of mankind. The doctrine offers great hope to a nation of people who groan under the yoke of tyrannical behavior by the State.

This book assumes that the reader already understands the dire condition of America. There have been countless books written over the last 20 years detailing America's demise, and the march towards tyranny via the Federal government. This book spends little time decrying darkness, rather this book is meant to bring hope and encouragement. It places within the hands of those concerned about our nation, a blueprint and means by which a stand can be made against a Federal government that has trampled our Constitution, assaults our person, liberty, and property, and impugns the law of God.

Americans are now nearly a completely conquered people. We do not have to sit by handwringing and passively submitting to our own destruction, however. The doctrine of the lesser magistrates provides a legitimate and proper means to restore order and resist tyranny. History has proven that peasant revolts are easily put down by the State. The lesser magistrate doctrine is effective in quelling abuses by the higher authority, and does so often without the shedding of blood.

This book is not, nor is it intended to be, a comprehensive or exhaustive declaration of the lesser magistrate doctrine. Rather, it is intended to be a primer. It is a starting place from which deeper study can be done by individuals. It is my hope that this book incites others to write further on this doctrine, and awakens people to deeper love and fear for God, and a greater vigilance to preserve liberty.

My prayer is that this book might be useful in stopping America's death march into tyranny and oppression, and point men back to Christ and His rule.

**Matthew Trewhella**
Epiphany 2013
**Milwaukee, Wisconsin**

# The Doctrine Defined

# Chapter 1

In 39 A.D., Publius Petronius, who was the Roman governor of Syria and Palestine, received an order from his superior, Caligula, the emperor of Rome. Caligula, who was convinced of his own divinity, ordered Petronius to assemble half his army and install an image of himself in the Jewish Temple at Jerusalem. Petronius had the statue of the emperor made in Sidon, and prepared his troops while he wintered in Ptolemais.

To the Jews, a statue of the emperor in the Temple was a severe affront to their religion. The Jews therefore sent numerous delegations during this time to protest before the governor concerning this law of the emperor. Petronius was so deeply moved by the reasoning of their protests that he wrote to Caligula that he would *not* enforce his order, and entreated the emperor to annul it.

When Emperor Caligula received the letter from Governor Petronius, he became outraged and ordered Petronius to commit suicide. Soon after however, Caligula was assassinated by his praetorian guards. Fortunately for Petronius, the ship carrying the order for him to commit suicide arrived *after* the ship carrying the news of the emperor's assassination.[5]

The statue never was placed in the Temple.

Though Governor Petronius would not have known it as such, he was practicing what would later be termed by Reformers such as John Calvin, Christopher Goodman, and John Knox, as *the doctrine of the lesser magistrates*. We call it a *doctrine* because it is a Christian doctrine first formalized by the pastors of Magdeburg, Germany. The word *magistrate* is an old term referring to any in civil government with authority, either elected or appointed.

---

5 Flavius Josephus, *The Works of Flavius Josephus* Book XVIII of the Antiquities, Ch. VIII, Vol.2, trans. William Whiston (Philadelphia, PA: Jas. B. Smith & Co., 94/1854) 85-89.

The lesser magistrate doctrine declares that when the superior or higher civil authority makes unjust/immoral laws or decrees, the lesser or lower ranking civil authority has both a right and duty to refuse obedience to that superior authority. If necessary, the lesser authorities even have the right and obligation to actively resist the superior authority.

For example, if Congress, the President, or the U.S. Supreme Court makes an unjust or immoral law or decree, a state legislature or governor could stand in defiance of their unjust law or decree and refuse to obey or implement it. Those lesser magistrates could, in fact, actively oppose such a law or decree. Even a city council or mayor could appropriately defy an unjust law or decree handed down by any higher authority.

A memorable statement that serves as a summary for the doctrine of the lesser magistrate actually came from a higher magistrate. Roman Emperor Trajan, while appointing a subordinate authority, handed him a sword and instructed him, saying, "Use this sword against my enemies, if I give righteous commands; but if I give unrighteous commands, *use it against me.*"[6]

Historically, this doctrine was practiced before the time of Christ and Christianity. But it was Christian men who formalized and embedded it into their political institutions throughout Western Civilization.

For example, the nobles who stood on the field of Runnymede in England to take King John's tyranny to task in the year 1215 were Christian men. These lesser magistrates forced the tyrant king to sign a treaty acknowledging certain rights for men. The *Magna Carta* stood in defiance of tyranny and oppression, and made clear that the state has limitations and that all are subject to the law, even government officials. That great document - Magna Carta - was the product of a Christian culture.

The Magna Carta played an important role in the historical process that led to the rule of constitutional law in the English-speaking world. Certain unjust and immoral actions by King John, along with his fiscal tyranny through taxation and fees, caused the nobles, who were functioning as lesser magistrates, to defy his higher authority. King John signed that document giving the people of England their cherished rights *only* because of the combined swords of the lesser magistrates who gathered to demand its signing.

6 Matthew Colvin, trans., *The Magdeburg Confession (1550)* (North Charleston, SC: Createspace Publishing, 2012) 72.

Calvin spoke of the lesser magistrate doctrine in his *Institutes of the Christian Religion* Amazingly, he did not appeal to Scripture in his support of it, rather he appealed to pagan historical examples.[7] But other Reformers did give a Scriptural foundation to the doctrine.

John Knox for example, in his *Appellation* written to the nobles of Scotland in 1558, cites over seventy passages of Scripture to support the doctrine. Knox insisted that the nobles, as lesser magistrates, were responsible to protect the innocent and oppose those who made unjust laws or decrees.[8]

The teaching by Christian men about the lesser magistrate, God's sovereignty, covenant, the nature of man, and church government shaped the views of Western Civilization that birthed constitutional governments.[9]

In what would become the United States, the lesser magistrate doctrine had a huge impact upon the thinking of our founders, and upon our nation's people regarding government and law. Today, however, neither the magistrates, nor the people, know of this doctrine as America's Pietistic-infected pulpits have long been silent regarding it.

If ever this nation needs to understand the lesser magistrate doctrine, it is now. The attacks upon the law of God are ferocious and relentless. The preborn are murdered and sodomy is proliferated. Immoral and unjust edicts are commonplace. The assault upon our freedom and liberties seems to be a daily undertaking by those in high office. But one thing has not changed; the lesser magistrate has a duty before God to uphold the good regardless of the new definitions of *"law"* created by the State.

Historically, the practice of the church has been that *when the State commands that which God forbids or forbids that which God commands, men have a duty to obey God rather than man.* The Bible clearly teaches this principle.[10] The lesser magistrate is to apply this principle to his office as magistrate. When an unjust decree is made by a higher authority, the lesser magistrate must choose to either join the higher magistrate

7 John Calvin, *Institutes of the Christian Religion* (1559) Book 4, Chapter 22, trans. Henry Beveridge (Peabody, MA: Hendrickson Publishing, 2008).

8 John Knox, *Selected Writings of John Knox*, edit. Kevin Reed (Dallas, TX: Presbyterian Heritage Publishing, 1558/1995) 471.

9 Douglas F. Kelly, *The Emergence of Liberty in the Modern World*, (Phillipsburg, NJ: P&R Publishing, 1992).

10 Exodus 1:15-21; Daniel 3; Daniel 6; Matthew 2:1-11; Acts 5:29

in his rebellion against God, or stand with God in opposition to the unjust or immoral decree.

The lesser magistrate doctrine is clearly founded in Scripture and seen in history, and, it is actively exercised in our day. In a later chapter, we will look at how lesser magistrates are utilizing their authority against Federal tyranny in our nation today, as well as look at the need for further action by the lesser magistrates in order to rein in a Federal government that has spurned its Constitutional restraints.

As our nation continues to sink into rebellion, immorality, and depravity, the lesser magistrate doctrine needs to be explained, both to the magistrates themselves and to the people of our country.

# Rooted in Interposition

# Chapter 2

The doctrine of the lesser magistrates is rooted in the historical, biblical doctrine of interposition. *Interposition* is that calling of God which causes one to step into the gap[11] - willingly placing oneself between the oppressor and his intended victim. Interposition is demonstrated when someone or some group interposes or positions themselves between an oppressor and the intended victim. This can be done verbally or physically.

The lesser magistrate demonstrates the doctrine of interposition by placing himself between the tyrant or bad law – and the people.

When Petronius defied Caligula, he was performing an act of interposition as a lesser magistrate on behalf of the Jews. To demonstrate his act of interposition, Petronius actually called the Jews to meet with him at Tiberias. When the Jews arrived, they were horrified to see Petronius' army – two legions – assembled before them.

The Jews stood on one side, while the army stood on the other. *Petronius stepped between them.* He then informed the Jews that this army was assembled under the authority of Emperor Caligula, who had ordered the army to war against and destroy them if resistance was made to having the image placed in the Temple. But then Governor Petronius went on to say:

> Yet I do not think it just to have such a regard to my own safety and honor, as to refuse to sacrifice them [his own safety and honor] for your preservation, who are so many in number, and endeavor to preserve the regard that is due your law; which as it has come down to you from your forefathers, so do you esteem it worthy of your utmost contention to preserve it. Nor, with the supreme assistance and power of God, will I

11 Ezekiel 22:27-31

> be so hardy as to suffer your temple to fall into contempt by the means of the imperial authority. I will, therefore, send to Caligula, and let him know what your resolutions arc, and will assist your suit as far as I am able, that you may not be exposed to suffer on account of the honest designs you have proposed to yourselves; and may God be your assistant, for His authority is beyond all the contrivance and power of men.[12]

Governor Petronius illustrated his interposition by standing between the emperor's soldiers and the Jews. He took a stand between the unjust law and the people. The interposition of the lesser magistrate requires a willingness to risk personal security for the sake of justice. Such risk is paramount to the lesser magistrate doctrine.

Scripture and history are loaded with acts of interposition.

In Exodus chapter one, Pharaoh ordered that all male Hebrew newborns should be killed by the mid-wives. The mid-wives refused to do so, and even employed deceit to cover their refusal to comply with his order. They *interposed* on behalf of these helpless babies, and stood in defiance of tyranny.[13]

In First Samuel chapter fourteen, King Saul made a foolish decree during a fierce battle, stating, "Cursed is the man who eats any food until evening, before I have taken vengeance on my enemies." His son, Jonathan, had not heard it and ate some honey. Saul was going to have him killed for eating it. But the Scripture says, all the people came to his defense and interposed on his behalf, declaring:

> Shall Jonathan die, who has accomplished this great deliverance in Israel? Certainly not! As the Lord lives, not one hair of his head shall fall to the ground, for he has worked with God this day. *So the people rescued Jonathan, and he did not die.*[14]

In the 4th century, the churchman Ambrose interposed on behalf of righteousness when he blocked the doors of the church to refuse Emperor Theodosius entry. Theodosius had unjustly killed 7,000 people in Thessalonica as reprisal for certain men in the city having killed

12 Josephus, *Works,* 85-89.

13 Exodus 1:15-22

14 I Samuel 14:24-45

some Roman officers. Ambrose stood in the doorway of the church and denied the emperor access until he publicly repented and made restitution.[15] Theodosius did repent and made restitution for his actions.

A recent example of interposition in history is the Romanian revolution of 1989. The revolution actually began in the city of Timisoara where Laszlo Tokes was the pastor of a Reformed church. The *Securitate* (secret police) came to arrest the pastor, a common occurrence in Ceausescu's Romania. Many of those arrested were never heard from again.

The people of the church learned of their pastor's impending arrest and gathered to blockade the doors of the church – *to interpose* – on his behalf and resist his arrest. The secret police sent to arrest Laszlo Tokes were accustomed to compliance. When the people blocked the doors, they were stunned by these actions, and merely parked their car down the street to wait the people out.

As word spread however, more and more people arrived to blockade access to the pastor. Within a few days, more than a thousand people had surrounded the church and would not leave. News of this spread to other areas and a nationwide revolution broke out. Two weeks later, Ceausescu and his wife lay dead on the palace steps. Their two-decade reign of terror was brought to an end. [16]

In America, an example of interposition took place in the late 1980's and early 1990's when tens of thousands of people were arrested at abortion clinics for blockading the doors – *interposing* – on behalf of the helpless preborn threatened with a brutal death. When the press questioned the legitimacy of such acts, they were informed by those involved that they were simply practicing the historic Christian doctrine of interposition.

When it comes to the interposition of the lesser magistrate, he interposes for the people as a whole – placing himself between the unjust laws or decrees of the higher authority and the people. He also acts in defense of the rule of law.

Daniel did this. When Daniel refused to obey the immoral decree of King Darius *not* to pray for thirty days, he not only acted as an individual

15 S.M. Houghton, *Sketches from Church History* (Carlisle, PA: Banner of Truth Trust, 1980) 24.

16 Laszlo Tokes, *The Fall of Tyrants* (Wheaton, IL: Crossway Books, 1990).

follower of the Lord, but also in his capacity as a lesser magistrate. *Remember, Daniel was one of three governors directly under Darius.*[17]

Daniel took an open stand in defiance of this unjust law. The Scripture says that "when Daniel knew that the writing was signed, he went home. And in his upper room, with his windows open towards Jerusalem, he knelt down on his knees three times that day, and prayed and gave thanks before his God."[18]

Notice he "knew" of the unjust law; his windows were "open" so all could see his non-compliance with the law; he "knelt down on his knees" so no one could mistake his defiance of the law; and he did it "three times" in one day to assure he would be seen.

For his act of interposition, Daniel was then thrown into the lion's den – willing to jeopardize his own life on behalf of the people as a whole, and to stand in defense of God's law and righteousness. Fortunately for Daniel, he lived to tell the story, as the rest is well-known history.[19]

The lesser magistrates act as a buffer for the people – placing themselves between the unjust laws or decrees of the higher authority and the people.

Historical American jurisprudence recognizes that the doctrine of the lesser magistrates is rooted in the doctrine of interposition. *Black's Law Dictionary* defines *interposition* as:

> The doctrine that a state, in the exercise of its sovereignty, may reject a mandate of the federal government deemed to be unconstitutional or to exceed the powers delegated to the federal government. The concept is based on the 10th Amendment of the Constitution of the United States reserving to the states powers not delegated to the United States.[20]

Not surprisingly, the U.S. Supreme Court ruled to reject the doctrine of interposition (though the particular case in which they did so was justified, expressly delegated powers should not have been ruled against completely as they were in the case).[21] The higher authority always wants

17 Daniel 6:2

18 Daniel 6:10

19 Daniel 6:21-23

20 Henry Campbell Black, *Black's Law Dictionary* (St. Paul, MN: West Publishing Co., 1978) 733.

21 Cooper v. Aaron, 358 U.S. 1 (1958). Also, Hunter Baker, *The End of Secularism* (Wheaton, IL: Crossway, 2009) 79.

to squelch any and all resistance to its authority. America's Founders, however, understood that acts of interposition were not dependent upon favorable rulings by the higher authority. The founding of our nation was an act of interposition by lesser magistrates, the *Declaration of Independence* being the pinnacle.

The legislatures of the colonies sent delegates to comprise the First and Second Continental Congresses. They represented the colonies. They were magistrates. The Declaration they wrote cited the offenses and tyranny of the upper-tier of British government – King George and the Parliament.

> This was especially necessary in light of the fact that the Parliament had no legitimate authority in the colonies because the colonies had been established by charters from the kings of England and were represented by their own legislatures. "No taxation without representation" referred to the fact that the colonies, unlike other realms of the British Empire, had no representation in Parliament and wanted none. But like the federal bureaucracies of today, Parliament had gradually assumed one power after another over a period of many decades, usurping authority from colony and King alike (often with the connivance of both – King and Parliament) thus becoming an overarching oppressor of the colonies.[22]

Patrick Henry, when he gave his famous "Give me liberty or give me death" speech, underscored the tyranny of England's Parliament, the hardened response of King George, and the need for the Continental Congress to interpose on behalf of the people. Henry stated:

> Sir, we have done everything that could be done to avert the storm which is now coming. We have petitioned; we have remonstrated; we have supplicated; we have prostrated ourselves before the throne, and have implored its *interposition* to arrest the tyrannical hands of the ministry and Parliament. Our petitions have been slighted; our remonstrances have

22 Wayne C. Sedlak. *Interposition: Revolt of the Lesser Magistrate*. Vision Viewpoint. 1997. Web. < http://visionviewpoint.com/pdfs/Interposition_of_the_lesser_magistrate.pdf>.

> produced additional violence and insults; our supplications have been disregarded and we have been spurned, with contempt, from the foot of the throne. In vain, after these things, may we indulge the fond hope of peace and reconciliation.[23]

Patrick Henry and his speech became famous precisely because he was a lesser magistrate in the Virginia legislature, the House of Burgesses. The common people rallied to the revolt of this lesser magistrate when he stood up and spoke.

Such interposition of the lesser magistrate provides action by duly constituted lawful authority. When individuals see immoral or unjust actions become law and policy in their nation, they desire to see the injustice corrected. The interposition of lesser magistrates provides the strength needed to resist a tyrant, and acts as a buffer for the common man, who might be persuaded to resist unlawful encroachments alone and by his own strength.

23 Patrick Henry; St. John's Church, Third Virginia Convention; March 23, 1775.

# ALL AUTHORITY IS DELE(

# CHAPTER 3

God is the ultimate authority. The Bible says plainly, "The Most High rules over the realm of mankind."[24] He gave His Law at Sinai. The very first decree is *"You shall have no other gods before Me."*[25] He created us, and thus knows best how we are to be governed. God is the ultimate Law-Giver[26] and Ruler.[27]

God has established four realms of government to which He delegates authority. They are: (1) self-government; (2) family government; (3) church government; and (4) civil government. Each has its own role, function, and jurisdiction. If one invades the jurisdiction of the other, chaos or tyranny ensues.

Each of these governments has positions of authority. Self-government's authority, of course, is the individual. In family government, the man is the head of the home. His wife acts as his co-regent, and both have authority over their children and property. In church government, there are the offices of elder, deacon, and pastor. In civil government, there are many and various positions of authority ranging from a policeman to the president.

The authority an individual possesses in any one of these four realms of government is *delegated* authority.[28] In other words, they derive their authority from God. Their authority is not autonomous or unconditional. Their authority is God-given, and thus, they have a duty to govern in accordance with His rule.[29]

A father (who has authority in family government) for example, should not tell his child to go rob the corner gas station because if caught

24 Daniel 4:17

25 Exodus 20:3

26 James 4:12

27 I Timothy 6:15

28 Colossians 1:16

29 Proverbs 8:15; Hosea 8:4

child will face less severe punishment than he. Rather, the father has duty before God to instruct the child in honesty and hard work, and to abhor theft. Hence, the father does not rule autonomously. He does not get to contradict the law of God just because he has a position of authority. The authority he has is *delegated* to him from God, and he has a duty therefore to govern his home in accordance with God's rule.

So it is with the civil government. Its power is not unlimited, nor is its rule to be autonomous. The word *autonomous* comes from two Greek words. *Autos* which means *self*, and *nomos* which means *law*. The authority of the State is *not* autonomous. They do not get to create law out of thin air or by whim. Men need to understand that the State is not God. They do not get to rule by mere fiat. They do not get to just "make up law as they go."

The authority of the State is limited. The authority it possesses is *delegated* authority from God. That the authority of the State is delegated from God is seen, among other places, in Romans 13. The first verse declares, *"For there is no authority except from God, and the authorities that exist are appointed by God."* Hence, the authority that the State possesses is delegated from God, and as such, they have a duty to govern in conformity with His rule.

America's Founders understood that the civil government's authority was delegated, and therefore, limited. They stated in the Declaration of Independence that all men "are endowed *by their Creator* with certain unalienable Rights, that among these are Life, Liberty, and the pursuit of Happiness." They understood that rights did not originate from the State, but rather were given to men by God.

Britain had ceased to rule and function within its God-ordained limits: therefore, America's colonists found themselves in conflict with her. The very next line of the Declaration states, "That to secure these rights, governments are instituted among men." Hence, when a government ceases to protect the citizenry of their God-given rights, but instead constructs laws attacking and depriving men of those rights, that government has perverted its power and has decided to play the tyrant. Such a government is to be resisted and not obeyed, regarding those areas of unjust laws.

John of Salisbury, in his monumental work *Policraticus*, written in 1159, taught that the State's authority was delegated authority. He writes:

> All power [authority] is from the Lord God; the power which the prince has is therefore from God, for the power of God is never lost nor severed from Him, *but He merely exercises it through a subordinate hand.*[30]

The State's authority is not autonomous, nor unlimited. Rulers are not to contravene - violate, oppose, or contradict - God's law. Citizens are not bound to hold unlimited obedience to the civil government.

In his writing, Salisbury states plainly that the king is a king precisely because he rules in the fear of the Lord, and according to His law. When the king makes law contrary to God's law, he becomes *a tyrant.*

What is tyranny? Salisbury wrote *"For tyranny is abuse of power entrusted by God to man."*[31] All authority, including civil authority, is delegated authority. When a higher authority makes unjust law, he abuses his power and may be resisted. When the lesser magistrate sees the higher magistrate make bad law, it is the right and duty of the lesser magistrate to interpose against such false law.

When the State authorities make law that contravenes or impugns the law of God, John Calvin wrote, *"For earthly princes lay aside their power when they rise up against God, and are unworthy to be reckoned among the number of mankind. We ought, rather, to spit upon their heads than to obey them."*[32]

Unfortunately, many people today are unconsciously schooled in *Statism.* They think the authority of the civil government *is* absolute and limitless. They think that rights and law originate with the State. An example of this is the United Nation's *Universal Declaration of Human Rights.* God is nowhere acknowledged in that Declaration. That's because Statists believe that the State is the originator of law and rights. Such thinking, however, stands in stark contrast to America's Declaration of Independence which recognizes rights are given of God to men.

Because Statism seems to have pervaded our culture down every avenue, including academia, the media, and public-policy, most politicians

---

30 John of Salisbury, *The Statesman's Book of John of Salisbury – Policraticus*, trans. John Dickinson (New York, NY: Russell & Russell, 1159/1963) 4.

31 Salisbury, *Policraticus*, 351.

32 *Commentary on Daniel*, Lecture XXX, Daniel 6:32

today *do believe* their authority is limitless; that they do rule by fiat; that they do get to create law out of thin air or by whim.

The lesser magistrate doctrine however, reminds the higher authority that their authority is delegated and limited. No man who holds state office rules with autonomy. The authority he has is delegated to him by God. Hence, all those in positions of authority stand accountable to God.

This standard is seen in all areas of government. In family government for example, if a husband tells his wife to murder his son or daughter, she has a duty not to obey. Also, if a husband decides to murder his son or daughter and forbids his wife to try and stop him, she has a duty to try and stop him anyway. So it is with the civil government: if the higher authority commands that which God forbids or forbids what God commands, the lesser magistrates must *not* obey, and if necessary actively resist.

The State is not God. The State's authority is not limitless. They don't get to do whatever just seems good to them. Men should not give unlimited obedience to civil government. In fact, men have a duty to oppose any in authority when they make unjust or immoral laws.

# The Duty of Lesser Magistrates

# Chapter 4

Duty is a word not often mentioned in our nation today. Expediency prevails. The path of least resistance is the path that most follow in our day, whether in private or public life. Commitment is a virtue long lost on Americans. Just consider the divorce rate if you doubt this.

Duty is that which a person owes to another, or by which a person is bound to another, by any natural, moral, or lawful obligation to perform. Duty is any action required by one's position or by moral or lawful considerations.

A magistrate is a person clothed with power as a public civil officer – whether executive, legislative, or judicial.[33] As the title implies, a lesser magistrate is one who possesses *less power* than a higher magistrate. For example, a county executive possesses less authority than a state governor. The position of the lesser magistrate can be obtained by election or by appointment.

The *primary duty* of the lesser magistrates regarding the doctrine of the lesser magistrates is threefold. First, they are to oppose and resist any laws or edicts from the higher authority that contravene the law or Word of God. Second, they are to protect the person, liberty, and property of those who reside within their jurisdiction from any unjust or immoral laws or actions by the higher authority. Third, they are not to implement any laws or decrees made by the higher authority that violate the Constitution, and if necessary, resist them.

They cannot hide behind the excuse "I'm just doing my job" or "I'm just following the law of the land" as an attempt to escape their duty. The duty of the lesser magistrate is to uphold that which is right in the sight of God, and to protect the people where his local authority or function resides. This is a sacred duty. We define it as sacred because it is founded in Scripture and proceeds from God.

---

33 Black, *Dictionary*, 857.

When we speak of *lesser* magistrates we are usually talking about a more *local* authority. Whatever the local authority may be, its jurisdiction is smaller than the higher authority that legislate an unjust or immoral decree. Whether a governor or a state legislature standing in defiance of the President or Congress or the Supreme Court, or whether a mayor or city council standing in defiance of the governor or Congress or state legislature, the authority of the lesser magistrate is more local than the higher magistrate.

Lesser magistrates are *not* to just unquestioningly do the bidding of the higher authority. State governments, for example, were never intended to be mere conduits or implementation centers for Federal government regulation, law, and policy as they have become today.

Hebert Schlossberg speaks to this point in his magnum opus, *Idols for Destruction*. He says regarding the lesser magistrates:

> The framers of the American Constitution were conscious of the excesses to which centralized political systems were prone, and their solution was to devise multiple levels of authority. The existence of states, cities, counties, townships, and independent taxing authorities, which, to apologists for the state, has been a messy derogation from beneficent centralized power, has saved us from some of the assaults on freedom that others have suffered.[34]

Schlossberg points out, however, that in our day these "*intermediate institutions, which formerly served to check the central power, have largely atrophied.*"[35] He later concludes:

> After three-quarters of a century, the new nationalism has borne bitter fruit. People who have despised the right of localities to govern themselves have delivered them into the hands of federal masters. Local politicians have acquiesced in the mugging of the provinces because in return for

34 Herbert Schlossberg, *Idols for Destruction: Christian Faith and Its Confrontation with American Society* (Nashville: Thomas Nelson Publishers, 1983) 213.

35 Schlossberg, *Idols*, 212.

> giving up political authority they have received monetary benefits.[36]

In other words, with the shekels come the shackles. The Federal master has bought the lesser magistrates off so they more readily do *its* bidding, rather than the peoples.' The lesser authorities become mere implementation centers of Federal policy.

The lesser magistrates in America today need to be reminded that a magistrate who upholds or follows an unjust or immoral law becomes complicit in the higher authorities' rebellion against God. Salisbury rightly declared in Policraticus:

> Loyal shoulders should sustain the power of the ruler *so long as it is exercised in subjection to God and follows His ordinances*; but if it resists and opposes the divine commandments, and wishes to make me share in its war against God, then with unrestrained voice, I answer back that *God must be preferred before any man on earth.*[37]

The resistance offered by lesser magistrates is wise and proper. Peasant revolts are easily put down by governments and suppressed. They lack the cohesion and order necessary to offer a successful resistance to tyranny by an organized central power. The following list[38] demonstrates why resistance by lesser magistrates is wise and necessary to turn back acts of tyranny by the higher authority:

1) Lesser magistrates already possess lawful, God-given authority which they may invoke.
2) Lesser magistrates have been supported by many in their successful bid to achieve office; therefore they have an established power base of popular support already in place.
3) Lesser magistrates usually have constitutional precedent and law on their side; so that, in other words, there is some heritage or history to which they can appeal.

---

36 Schlossberg, *Idols*, 214.

37 Salisbury, *Policraticus*, 258.

38 This is a modified list from original. Wayne C. Sedlak, *Interposition: Revolt of the Lesser Magistrate.* Vision Viewpoint. 1997. Web.

4) Lesser magistrates already have access to a public forum by which they can articulate the particulars of the grievances involved.
5) Lesser magistrates, by virtue of their office, are able to address the pangs of conscience, doubt, and indecision of the people when they see tyranny developing in their nation and see the need for resistance. People respond to honorable and authoritative leadership, so they recognize the lesser magistrates' God-given authority to resist unjust and immoral law and can rally behind them.
6) Lesser magistrates can provide relief and refuge, protection and support for the distressed more readily than can ordinary individuals, becoming, by their office, an instrument of temporal deliverance/salvation for the distressed. This is institutionalized deliverance, a theme reiterated in Scripture repeatedly.
7) Lesser magistrates can strike terror into the hearts of oppressors, flushing them out into the open and exposing them for promoting what is evil; even as they attack the lesser magistrate's position in office, and further their injustice.
8) Lesser magistrates have the best chance of resolving injustice without upheaval or bloodshed. A tyrannical government is less anxious to push their oppression if they know that the opposition has the proper leadership and order of lesser magistrates. When the lesser magistrates refuse to comply with unjust or immoral law, the matter can often be resolved in favor of what is right without armed revolution or bloodshed being necessary.
9) God declares a willingness to support such magistrates in their capacity and office,[39] as they represent what God instituted government to be – a picture of true justice to the culture and citizenry at large and an empowered and proper deliverance against the onslaughts of oppression and evil. Such a position gives people hope and a foundation upon which to erect a just and upright system of constitutional protections and proper "due process" of law as bulwarks against tyranny.

Lesser magistrates, by virtue of their office, constitute lawful authority. When the lesser magistrate stands against unjust or immoral law

39 Romans 13:1-4

made by a superior, his actions benefit those under his jurisdiction, as well as the nation as a whole.

Simply put, the lesser magistrates provide order when the superior authority acts unjustly or immorally and its abuse of power needs to be quelled.

# THE OBJECTIVE STANDARD FOR LAW

# CHAPTER 5

Disobeying authority is no trifling matter. *When* to disobey should not be left to the whims of mere men. There needs to be an objective standard to determine if a law is moral or immoral, just or unjust. There must be an objective standard to know if a law is right or wrong.

For nearly 1500 years throughout Western Civilization the objective standard was the law of God. This fact was acknowledged by writers in the West for hundreds of years.

Salisbury made clear that *God's law* was the *objective standard* for all of Western Civilization. All, whether king or commoner, were accountable to the "higher law" - the law of God.[40]

God's moral law as the "higher law" provides an objective standard whereby one is able to discern right from wrong, or good from evil. The "higher law" exists independent of the authority of any government, and all governments of men are accountable to it. *The tyrant State abhors an objective standard to which it is accountable, rather it flourishes in a subjective environment.* It wants to be accountable to no one.

William Blackstone (1723-1780) is the most cited legal scholar in the writings of America's Founding Fathers. He was a British jurist who wrote a four-volume work entitled *Commentaries on the Laws of England* (1766). His Commentaries are the bedrock of American jurisprudence.

Like Salisbury, Blackstone said this "higher law" is God's law. Blackstone referred to God's law as "those superior laws," and stated that "upon these two foundations, the law of nature and the law of revelation [God's written law], depend all human laws; that is to say, no human laws should be suffered to contradict these."[41]

40 Salisbury, *Policraticus*, 33.

41 William Blackstone, *Commentaries on the Laws of England*, Vol.1 (Philadelphia, PA: Childs & Peterson, 1765/1860) 42.

We can be sure that when Blackstone spoke of "*those superior laws*" that "*no human laws should be suffered to contradict*," he was speaking of God's law as revealed in the Bible. He went on to write:

> It is binding over all the globe in all countries, and at all times: no human laws are of any validity, if contrary to this; and such of them as are valid derive all their force and all their authority, mediately or immediately, from this original. The doctrines thus delivered we call the revealed or divine law, and they are found *only in the Holy Scriptures*.[42]

Blackstone went on to say, "Man, considered as a creature, must necessarily be subject to the laws of his Creator, for he is entirely a dependent being." Blackstone was simply acknowledging what Western Man knew to be true – that the law of God was the objective standard for Western Civilization. Like John of Salisbury 600 years earlier, Blackstone viewed God's law as the "higher law" to whom all men and all governments of men were accountable.

James Wilson (1742-1798) was a signer of the Declaration of Independence, a major force in the drafting of the U.S. Constitution, and one of the original justices appointed to the United States Supreme Court by George Washington. Like Blackstone, he said the following about law:

> As promulgated by reason and the moral sense, it has been called natural; as promulgated by the holy scriptures, it has been called revealed law. As addressed to men, it has been denominated the law of nature; as addressed to political societies, it has been denominated the law of nations. But it should always be remembered, that this law, whether natural or revealed, made for men or for nations; flows from the same divine source: *it is the law of God*.[43]

Wilson went on to say, "Human law must rest its authority, ultimately, upon the authority of that law, which is divine."[44]

---

42 Blackstone, *Commentaries*, 42.

43 James Wilson, *The Works of James Wilson*, Vol.1, edit. James Dewitt Andrews (Chicago, IL: Callaghan and Company, 1792/1896) 92-93.

44 Wilson, *Works*, 93.

If there is no objective standard to judge the purpose and limits of the State, then the State can do whatever it pleases because the people will not know any different. *If a citizenry does not know the purpose, functions, and limitations of the State, then the State can do whatever it wants to do because the citizenry doesn't realize anything improper is being done.* For there to be any indignation towards acts of tyranny by the State, one must be able to identify tyranny.

The law of God is that objective standard so that men know when governments are making unjust or immoral law.

When an objective standard is thrown off, law is easily and constantly *redefined* by the State and society. Man's passions and desires begin to determine what is "lawful." Man makes himself the standard, and because of the nature of man, the standard changes all of the time. For this reason, an objective standard of law is always and everywhere necessary; one which does *not* change, and which is applicable to all mankind.

Unfortunately, many today believe there is no objective standard to which the governments of men are accountable. The results are disastrous. Good becomes redefined as evil and evil becomes redefined as good. A person who might try to protect a preborn child from death spends the night in jail, while an abortionist who murdered that helpless child goes home and sips martinis next to his fireplace.

What every society needs is the moral law of God. His law is an objective standard. His law is objective truth. He is the Creator of all. He best knows how we are to be governed. He declares what is right and what is wrong. His law/truth is not subjective, rather it is objective.

When the higher magistrate or authority makes laws which clearly contravene the law or Word of God, the lesser magistrate therefore has a right and duty to act in defiance of that unjust or immoral law. This is because the objective standard to which all men and all governments of men are accountable has been impugned.

*The disobedience of the lesser magistrate is not subjective.* He is only justified in defying the higher authority when the higher authority clearly contravenes the law of God, or makes law which is clearly an attack upon the person, liberty, or property of the people in the lesser magistrate's jurisdiction, or makes law or policy which violates the Constitution.

# The Rule of Law and the Lesser Magistrates

# Chapter 6

When Jesus said *"Render unto Caesar the things that are Caesar's, and to God the things that are God's,"*[45] He was making clear that the civil government has limitations. The State is not the "be all and end all." It cannot declare just anything to be its own. They cannot make up law as they go, nor change the immutable laws of God. The authority they have is delegated to them from God – it is not autonomously held.

Early Christian men took a stand and defied the State when it crossed its limitations. As a result, many early Christians suffered martyrdom because they would not obey a State that had exceeded its God-given authority. They also constructed *thought* as to how a godly society should be structured. The persuasion of their thinking resulted in Christians overturning the greatest empire of the world – Rome.[46] From there Christianity, which breeds liberty, spread across the western world freeing nations from the tyranny of the strongest and most brutal. Christianity established the "rule of law" in Western Civilization.

The rule of law simply stated is: *the law is king.* All are subject to the laws of the land, both king and commoner, both government officials and citizens, and that law is equitable to all.

Whose law or what law does the rule of law consist of?

God's law was the standard by which the rule of law was established for Western Civilization. His law was viewed as the "higher law" to which all men and all governments of men were accountable. The rule of law is a Western Civilization phenomenon fueled by Christianity.

The Greeks spoke of the rule of law, and tried to implement it, though with limited success. But Christian men in the West recognized a transcendent law found in the Scriptures. They formalized God's moral law,

45 Matthew 22:21

46 Acts 17:6

along with biblical principles of authority and government, under what became known as "the rule of law."

*The rule of law is crumbling in America and throughout the West today.* Fifty years ago, abortion was illegal and most of society thought the prospect of murdering their own son or daughter in the womb to be abhorrent. Now it is considered a right by law to do so, with much of society indifferent towards it.

Just twenty years ago, homosexual acts were illegal; most of society considered it filthy behavior. Now it is decriminalized and paraded down the streets of America without even a whimper from the populace. Rather, many Americans now cheer homosexuals on, as the churches sit by in silence or are busy rewriting 2000 years of biblical interpretation in order to accommodate the acceptance of homosexuality.

No-fault divorce, the decriminalization of adultery, the phalanx of laws created by the State to invade our domestic affairs, disarm the people, seize our property, and harass our persons – all point to the crumbling rule of law in America.

Christian thinker and author, Francis Schaeffer, once said "If there are no absolutes by which to judge society, then society becomes an absolute."[47] This is what is happening to the rule of law in America today. The State and society – which are ever changing – substitute their own reasoning as the standard of law. Objective truth is anathema.

A just government rules in the fear of the Lord.[48] Over the last several decades however, America appears to have thrown the law of God under the bus. America has spurned the rule of God. There has been what appears to be an intentional, systematic effort by the State, academicians, and certain wealthy men to ridicule, undermine, and set aside God's law as the rule of law for America. Even American Christianity, with its embrace of Pietism, has spurned the law of God. The result is the rule of law is crumbling in America.

And people see it. They may not understand that it's the rule of law crumbling, but they intuitively know that something is wrong with our nation. Already the talk has begun. Fear and concern is descending on Americans.

---

47 Francis Schaeffer, *How Shall We Then Live?_The Rise and Decline of Western Thought and Culture* (Old Tappan NJ: Fleming H Revell Company, 1976) 224.

48 2 Samuel 23:3

Barely a month goes by where you watch the news and don't see another lawless act by our Federal government. They think they have no limitations. They think they're above the law. They force Americans to be ruled by bureaucracies that are immune from the law, and allow no remedy at law to rein them in so citizens can protect themselves.

When people see those in authority as no longer upholding the law, but rather as perverting the law, they will only endure it so long before they go in one of two directions. They will either take action against the State, or they will accommodate and adjust themselves to the state of things, working "the system" to their own personal benefit. For the latter, conforming and lying low in hope that one's own ox isn't gored becomes the prevalent mindset.

As this begins to happen, anarchy and brute force lie ahead for Western Man. Man fails to realize that in refusing to be governed by God, he ends up being ruled by tyrants. Because man wants to throw off the law of God - the civil government then has the green light to make up law on whim. Those in power arrogantly redefine right and wrong, truth and error, good and evil. Because man wants to throw off the law of God - only misery and despair lie ahead for Western Man.

The law of God has been attacked by people holding power, whether statists, socialists, politicians, scientists, scholars, academicians, entertainers, egalitarians, educators or pastors. Man arrogantly desires to be a law unto himself, despising the law of God. So the rule of law in Western Civilization, having been based upon the law of God, is now crumbling.

*How does the rule of law relate to the lesser magistrates?* As America (and all the West) crumbles because it has spurned the law of God as the rule of law, we will be presented with an opportunity when godly lesser magistrates will need to stand in the gap. They will need to interpose for the sake of the rule of law, for the sake of the people they represent, and defy bad law.

Present day magistrates need to know of the lesser magistrate doctrine so that conscience prods them more vigorously in their duty and responsibility in the sight of God. They will then be prepared to act in defense of the people they represent. The people also need to understand the lesser magistrate doctrine, so that when the lesser magistrates stand, they will rally around them, and not let them hang there, left blowing in the wind.

When the lesser magistrates act, there will be those who will accuse them of anarchy and chaos. Because Americans have heard the mantra their entire lives that "We are a nation of law – we must respect the rule of law" many may tend to believe the accusations. But what if unjust or tyrannical law has been made? Are we to respect it just because the State declares it to be *"the law of the land?"* Are we to passively stand by and conform?

Western history exclaims a resounding – "No!" From Thomas Aquinas who declared that "an unjust law is no law at all" to the Nuremburg Trials where unquestioned obedience to man's law was soundly condemned – Western history points out our duty to disobey when ordered to do that which is unjust or wrong, even when the civil government has made it legal. As America's founders were known to say, "Disobedience to tyrants is obedience to God."

*The duty to resist unjust law is the product of Christian thought.* Our loyalty is to Christ first - not man, not the State. So when the civil government makes unjust or immoral laws or policies, we obey Christ, not the State. Christianity acts as a check to tyranny. The whole of society should be thankful for the preservation of liberty that Christianity engenders. Christians are the best of citizens. We obey the State and are productive in commerce. We disobey the State only when they make unjust or immoral law. We have a salvific affect upon society as a whole.

When Christians practiced civil disobedience by blockading the doors of America's abortion clinics in the early 1990's in an attempt to protect the preborn from a brutal death, they were accused of anarchy and chaos, and admonished to respect the rule of law. The truth is the U.S. Supreme Court instigated anarchy and chaos when they declared preborn babies open game to those who would kill-for-profit in their 1973 Roe v. Wade decision. Those blockading the doors were actually tying to restore order.

The U.S. Supreme Court was the anarchist, not the pro-lifers.

When the lesser magistrates are accused of insubordination or anarchy because they interpose against bad law, the counterfeit man-made "rule of law" will be heralded by the Statists. They will sing and herald the mantra – "we must obey the rule of law!" But if the rule of law itself is unjust and immoral, then what virtue is there in supporting it? To do so is to stand the true rule of law on its head.

Men should not respect "the rule of law" just because "it's the rule of law," rather we respect it because as Blackstone said - it does not *"contradict"* the law of God. This is why Western Civilization respected the rule of law for nearly 1500 years, precisely because it was based upon the law of God.

# Magdeburg and the Lesser Magistrates

# Chapter 7

Martin Luther was rescued from death by the interposition of a lesser magistrate who defied the order of his superior. From the time Luther pounded his "Ninety-Five Theses" to the church door in Wittenberg in 1517, there were religious and political forces that opposed what he stood for and wanted him dead.

Prince Frederick the Wise was the Elector of Saxony, and as such, he was a lesser magistrate. His superior, Emperor Charles V, had ordered Luther to defend himself against the charge of heresy in Worms, Germany, in the spring of 1521. Through Frederick's efforts, Luther was guaranteed safe-conduct so that he could personally answer charges and renounce or reaffirm his theological views. Luther therefore attended what became known as the Diet of Worms.

When Luther failed to renounce his beliefs and submit to Roman Catholic rule, Emperor Charles V ordered Luther's "apprehension." Charles forbade "anyone from this time forward to dare, either by words or by deeds, to receive, defend, sustain, or favor the said Martin Luther"[49] and commanded that the reformer be brought before his court for punishment as a "notorious heretic." Such language was tantamount to a death sentence.

Though directly under Charles' authority, Prince Frederick did *not* arrest Luther and turn him over to Charles as ordered. Instead, he feigned Luther's abduction in order to hide and protect him. He used his lesser authority to countermand Emperor Charles' unjust order and defend Luther, who resided in his jurisdiction.

This act of interposition by this lesser magistrate had far-reaching implications for the future of the Reformation. Thirty years later, the protection afforded Luther by a lesser magistrate clearly had an impact on the

49 Edict of Worms, May 25, 1521.

men of Magdeburg, Germany. Emperor Charles V imposed his Augsburg Interim on May 15, 1548. This law was an attempt to force Protestants back under traditional Roman Catholic beliefs, practices, and rule.

Only one city in all of Germany stood against the Interim – *Magdeburg.* In that city, the magistrates protected the people and defied political and religious tyranny. They upheld God's law, Word, and Gospel. While all the rest of Christendom went along with the Interim's sanctions in order to preserve their own well-being, the lone city which stood in opposition was the outlawed Magdeburg.

As tensions mounted, the pastors of Magdeburg wrote a defense of their position for standing in defiance of Charles V and his unjust Interim. They published their *Confession and Defense of the Pastors and Other Ministers of the Church of Magdeburg* in April, 1550. This document later became referred to simply as "The Magdeburg Confession."[50]

The magistrates of Magdeburg refused to submit to the emperor. Their consciences were resolute because of their fealty to Christ and their understanding of His Word, and they stood their ground because they understood the doctrine of the lesser magistrates.

In October of 1550, Charles' forces surrounded the city. The people of Magdeburg burned everything outside the city walls and closed the gates. The siege of Magdeburg had begun.

The Magdeburg Confession is an important historical work because the pastors of Magdeburg were the first in the history of mankind to set forth in a doctrinal format what only later came to be known as the doctrine of the lesser magistrates. Though many men acted in accordance with this doctrine prior to Christ (showing that this doctrine is not only found in special revelation but also in general revelation, also referred to as "nature"), and though many Christian men acted in accordance with it subsequent to Christ's time on earth, it wasn't formalized as a doctrine until the Reformers of the 16th century made it such.

Other Christian men who wrote of such matters prior to the Reformation include John of Salisbury and Azo in the 12th century.[51] But the pastors of Magdeburg were the first in history to identify many historical examples of the lesser magistrate doctrine in action, both from the Bible and from extra-biblical sources. They wrote in the Confession

50 Matthew Colvin, trans., *The Magdeburg Confession (1550)* (North Charleston, SC: Createspace Publishing, 2012) 72.

51 Kelly, *Emergence of Liberty,* 30.

that they were prodded by their difficult circumstances into formalizing a doctrine rarely articulated. They write:

> We would have desired even now to hide this true opinion as it had always been hidden hitherto, had we not been defeated by the present injustice and tyranny of certain men, and deemed that the preservation of the Gospel and the True Church ought to be put before such dangers from those ignorant men.[52]

The "true opinion" that had "always been hidden hitherto" is the doctrine of the lesser magistrates. These pastors were the first to write down the doctrine as proven sound in Scripture and practiced in history.

The first name affixed at the end of the Magdeburg Confession is Nicholas von Amsdorff.[53] He was a close friend of Martin Luther, and accompanied him to his hearing at Worms in 1521. He was also with Luther on the return trip when Prince Frederick "kidnapped" Luther (of which Amsdorff was privy) in order to hide and protect him. Amsdorff remained a close friend until Luther's death in 1546.

The Magdeburg Confession consists of three parts. The first part is designed to assure the Magdeburg magistrates of the confessors' orthodoxy that they stood doctrinally with Luther. Therefore, they laid out in detail their Lutheran theology. The third part is a warning and exhortation to all those that would take actions against them, whether directly or through complicity, as well as those who would stand by and do nothing to help them. Much wisdom is declared in that section.

The second part of the Confession, however, lays out the lesser magistrate doctrine. This section begins with an appeal to Charles V. The pastors exhort him to remove those surrounding him who give him bad counsel. They make clear to Charles that the *only* reason for this impasse is due to his attack upon their Christian faith; that when those in civil authority make law which impugns the law or Word of God, Christian men have a duty to obey God, rather than men.

They also assure Charles that they are his best citizens. They write:

52 Colvin, *Magdeburg Confession*, 72.

53 Colvin, *Magdeburg Confession*, 86.

> We will give from our Churches the greatest possible number of men who, if they be able to enjoy their own religion through you, will declare their obedience toward you in all owed and upright duties, and loyalty without hypocrisy... perhaps more than all those whom you say are obedient to you.[54]

They declare they have taken their stand against him only because of their love for Christ, and His law and Word. Therefore their stand is sure, and they tell Charles, "*We are not swayed by the majesty or wealth of anyone.*"[55] The pastors then introduce their formal presentation of the lesser magistrate doctrine - "*this doctrine which we hand down about the legitimate defense of the lower magistrate against a superior.*"[56]

They proceed to make three distinct arguments, which include a list of examples both from Scripture and from history. The pastors commence their arguments by stating:

> The Magistrate is an ordinance of God for the honor to good works, and a terror to evil works (Romans 13). Therefore when he begins to be a terror to good works and honor to evil, there is no longer in him, because he does thus, the ordinance of God, but the ordinance of the devil. And he who resists such works, does not resist the ordinance of God, but the ordinance of the devil.[57]

Hence, when a superior magistrate perverts his God-given function and begins to uphold evil and to be a terror against good, the lesser magistrates under his authority must decide to either join the unjust magistrate in his rebellion against God, or, as the pastors say, "*vindicate the honor of God*"[58] and obey Him rather than man.

In their arguments, the pastors declare the idea of unlimited obedience to the State as "*an invention of the devil.*"[59] They rightly assert that all authority is delegated from God. Therefore, if the one in authority makes commands contrary to the law or Word of God, those subject to

---

54 Colvin, *Magdeburg Confession*, 52.

55 Colvin, *Magdeburg Confession*, 49.

56 Colvin, *Magdeburg Confession*, 54.

57 Colvin, *Magdeburg Confession*, 57.

58 Colvin, *Magdeburg Confession*, 65.

59 Colvin, *Magdeburg Confession*, 68.

his authority have both a right not to obey, and a duty to actively resist. The pastors proffer an example from family government. They write:

> Let us take an example concerning a father of a family. If he should come to his wife or grown daughters in his house with some scoundrels in an obvious attempt to prostitute them, then his wife and daughters not only would not render their husband and father the obedience they otherwise owe him, but when they are not able to preserve their chastity in any other way, they would drive him off with stones.[60]

The pastors then take this example and make an analogy to civil government. Their point is that no one in authority – whether in family, church, or civil government – holds his authority autonomously. Rather it is delegated to them from God. If the authority therefore makes law which contravenes the law of God, those subject to their authority can refuse obedience because, as the pastors write, *"divine laws necessarily trump human ones."*[61]

To the pastors of Magdeburg, *all* magistrates, higher and lower, possess delegated authority from God. Therefore, the lesser magistrates have a right and duty to oppose the superior magistrate-turned-tyrant when he makes laws contrary to the law and Word of God.

The pastors did not view unjust or immoral laws and edicts by the higher magistrate to be an *excuse* for lesser magistrates *not* to protect the citizens of their jurisdiction. Rather they viewed resistance to unjust or immoral laws and edicts by the higher magistrate as the *duty* of the lesser magistrates in order *to* protect the citizens within their jurisdiction.[62]

The pastors are so detailed in their Confession that they carefully define four *levels* or *degrees* of tyranny by a superior magistrate, and the legitimate and proper response of the lesser magistrates to each. There was order to their resistance. Their position was well thought-out, adhered to standards, and appealed to immutable truth.

These Lutherans were *first* to set forth a doctrine on the lesser magistrate. The Confession set forth a biblical and historical foundation that

---

60 Colvin, *Magdeburg Confession*, 64.

61 Colvin, *Magdeburg Confession*, 63.

62 David Mark Whitford, *Tyranny and Resistance: The Magdeburg Confession and the Lutheran Tradition* (St. Louis, MO: Concordia Publishing House, 2000) 100.

strengthened the consciences of the magistrates in Magdeburg to resist the unjust law of Charles V. Its implications went far beyond Magdeburg, however.

Their writings clearly impacted other of the Reformers in Europe, including John Knox, Theodore Beza, Philipp Mornay, and Christopher Goodman – all four of whom went on to further build the doctrine of the lesser magistrates.

The influence of the Magdeburg Confession upon John Knox was seen during a debate in 1564 with William Maitland of Lethington, who was Secretary of State for Mary, Queen of Scots. Maitland chided Knox for his position that lesser magistrates and the people could oppose the higher authority. He stated of Knox's position, "I think ye shall not have many learned men of your opinion."

Knox replied:

> My lord, the truth ceases not to be the truth, howsoever it be that men either misknow it, or yet gainstand it. And yet, I praise my God, I lack not the consent of God's servants in that head.[63]

Knox then handed a copy of the Magdeburg Confession to the Secretary and bid him to read the names of the pastors signed at the end of the document declaring the just defense of the city. Then he added, "To resist a tyrant, is not to resist God, nor yet His ordinance."

After looking at the names of the pastors, Lethington mockingly stated, "Men of no note." Upon which Knox replied of the Magdeburgers, "Yet servants of God."

John Calvin's successor, Theodore Beza, when writing of the right and duty of lesser magistrates to resist superior authority which makes unjust laws or orders, said of Magdeburg, "The city of Magdeburg, situated on the Elbe, offered the outstanding example of this in our own time."[64]

Twenty years later, while writing *On the Right of Magistrates* in 1574, Beza included in the title itself "*A Treatise Published by Those in*

63 John Knox, *History of the Reformation in Scotland*, edit. William Dickinson, Vol.2 (New York, NY: Philosophical Library, 1566/1950) 129-130.

64 Theodore Beza, *On the Punishment of Heretics*, 1554.

*Magdeburg in 1550.*"[65] Beza first published his work anonymously due to the political situation at that time, and he thought so highly of and was so deeply influenced by the Magdeburgers, that he ascribed his writing to them.

The Magdeburg Confession is of vast historical significance precisely because it laid out the lesser magistrate doctrine from Holy Scripture and history.

The siege of Magdeburg lasted for over a year from 1550-1551. About 4000 of Charles' forces were killed, while 468 Magdeburgers lost their lives. The siege ended on November 4, 1551 with favorable terms for the Magdeburgers – they were free to practice their Christian faith.

If not for the actions of the Magdeburgers, the entire Reformation itself may very well have been a blip on the radar screen of human history. Charles had intended to re-Romanize all of the Empire. However, the actions of these reformers clearly led to two very important councils and subsequent treaties.

After the siege ended, Maurice of Saxony left Magdeburg, and along with other German princes attacked Charles and drove him out of Germany and into Italy. Charles V, weary of civil war, granted religious freedom to the Reformers at the Peace of Passau in August of 1552, just nine months after the siege of Magdeburg had ended.

The Peace of Passau granted peace only until another Imperial Diet could be held. That Diet was held in Augsburg in 1555. The result was the Peace of Augsburg (Sept. 25, 1555) which declared – *cuius regio, eius religio* ("whosoever region, his religion").

Prior to and during the siege of Magdeburg, the pastors and other ministers wrote over 200 pamphlets that set forth a defense of their actions. These pamphlets were printed by the thousands and distributed not only throughout Germany, but also throughout the Holy Roman Empire, England, Scotland, and France.[66]

Greatest of all – the siege of Magdeburg produced the *Magdeburg Confession*, which is the earliest known historical document to formalize the doctrine of the lesser magistrates.

---

65 Theodore Beza, *On the Right of Magistrates*, 1574. trans. Henry-Louis Gonin, ed. Patrick S. Poole. <http://www.constitution.org/cmt/beza/magistrates.htm>

66 Oliver Olson, *Theology of Revolution: Magdeburg 1550-1551*, The Sixteenth Century Journal, Vol.3, No.1 (Apr. 1972) 56-79.

# John Knox, Holy Scripture, and the Lesser Magistrates

# Chapter 8

John Knox, the champion of the Reformation in Scotland, who was known "to fear no man" and who hazarded his life declaring the truth of God's Word, demonstrated in his *Appellation* that the doctrine of the lesser magistrates is thoroughly biblical. He built upon what the Magdeburg pastors had produced in their Confession.

Knox's Appellation, which was written in December of 1558 to Scotland's nobles, is the best treatise ever written on the doctrine of the lesser magistrates. The nobles were the lesser magistrates of that day, and Knox wrote to them in their capacity as such.

Knox wrote his Appellation (Appeal) because the Roman Catholic Church had condemned him and burned him in effigy. He wrote to declare to the nobles, *as lesser magistrates*, their responsibility to protect the innocent and oppose those who made unjust decrees.

Knox had written to them 14 months earlier, wherein he told them that their chief duty "is to vindicate and deliver your subjects and brethren from all violence and oppression, to the uttermost of your power."[67] Two months later he wrote them again, stating they had an obligation to "defend your brethren from persecution and tyranny, be it against princes or emperors, to the utmost of your power."[68]

He repeats in his Appellation that those under their care are "to be defended from all oppression and tyranny."[69] Knox saw the lesser magistrate had not only the function, but the *duty* to interpose against oppression and tyranny, and act as a buffer between unjust law and the people.

---

67 John Knox, *Selected Writings of John Knox*, edit. Kevin Reed (Dallas, TX: Presbyterian Heritage Publishing, 1558/1995) 471.

68 Knox, *Selected Writings*, 368.

69 Knox, *Selected Writings*, 488.

Knox insisted that lesser magistrates have a duty to resist the tyranny of superior magistrates when the superior magistrate exceeds his God-given authority or actually makes declarations which are in rebellion to the law of God.

He exhorts the nobles in his Appellation:

> You are bound to correct and repress whatsoever you know him (the higher magistrate) to attempt expressly repugning to God's word, honour, glory, or what you shall espy him to do against his subjects great or small.[70]

The first text of Scripture that Knox cites is Jeremiah 26:10-16. In this passage, the false priests and prophets have condemned Jeremiah to death. The princes of Judah (the lesser magistrates), hear of this and come to the house of the Lord so they can hear what the priests and prophets have to say. Jeremiah is then allowed to speak in his defense, wherein he tells the lesser magistrates the same things for which the false priests and prophets had condemned him to death. The lesser magistrates then interpose on behalf of Jeremiah by adjudicating that *"this man does not deserve to die."*[71]

Knox chose this passage because the Protestant faith was under attack by church officials from Rome. They were using the arm of the State to persecute him and others. So this was a perfect text for Knox to employ in order to encourage the nobles to exercise their authority as lesser magistrates, both in his defense, and the defense of others.

Often one does not notice things in Scripture until a real life situation brings it to the foreground out of necessity. Such was obviously the case with Knox. He goes on to build his doctrine in which he cites more than seventy passages of Scripture.

Knox appeals to Daniel chapter three. King Nebuchadnezzar made an unjust law commanding all people to worship an image he had built. Three of Daniel's friends, men who feared God, refused to worship the idol. As punishment, they were then thrown into a flaming furnace to be burned alive, but God delivered them.

What is important to note is that, though they acted in fealty to God as individuals, *they also acted in the capacity of lesser magistrates.* Verse

70 Knox, *Selected Writings,* 504-505

71 Jeremiah 26:16

twelve makes clear that these three men had positions of authority in the Babylonian kingdom. They not only stood against this unjust law as individuals because of their faithfulness to the Lord, but they interposed on behalf of the people as lesser magistrates.

Notice their defiance to this unjust law. It was theologically-driven. They respond to Nebuchadnezzar's threats of the furnace by saying:

> O Nebuchadnezzar, we have no need to answer you in this matter. If that is the case [him throwing them into the fiery furnace], our God is able to deliver us from the burning fiery furnace, and He will deliver us from your hand, O king. But if not, *let it be known to you, O king, that we do not serve your gods, nor will we worship the gold image which you have set up.*[72]

Notice their stand was *theocentric.* What made them understand that this was an unjust law was that it stood in opposition to God's law, and as followers of the Lord, and as lesser magistrates, they had a duty to disregard it, and stand in defiance of it.

Knox also brings up Daniel chapter six wherein Daniel and all King Darius' subjects were ordered by "royal statute" not to pray. Daniel opened his windows and prayed anyway, again, not only out of concern that he would honor and remain obedient to the Lord as an individual, but also in the capacity of a lesser magistrate.[73] He too acted as a buffer between unjust law and the people.

In another case, Knox cites Second Kings chapter eleven, and points out that Jehoiada, the churchman of the time, calls upon and acts in conjunction with the captains of the guard, who are lesser magistrates, to restore order in the kingdom and depose the wicked tyrant, Queen Athaliah.

In a lengthy passage, Knox cites Jeremiah 36:9-31 to impress upon the nobles of Scotland just how grave and important their duty as lesser magistrates is to secure just law and peace in the land. In this passage, Jeremiah has written a prophecy regarding the doom of Jerusalem by Babylon. He has his assistant, Baruch, read the prophecy in the house of

72 Daniel 3:16-18

73 Daniel 6:2

the Lord. The princes (lesser magistrates) hear of its reading and have Baruch come and read it to them, as well.

Upon hearing the prophecy, the Scripture says of the princes "they looked in fear one to another."[74] They feared not only because of the impending judgment, but also because they knew that King Jehoiakim would be outraged by such a pronouncement, as he was bent on fighting against Babylon.

They told Baruch that he and Jeremiah should go hide and let no one know where they are, while they would go to reveal the prophecy to the king. Sure enough, the king responded negatively to the prophecy. He cut it with a knife and burned it in the fire of his hearth.[75]

Knox points out to the nobles of Scotland that the response of the princes of Judah as lesser magistrates was that they did *not* interpose. The Scripture says that upon seeing the king cut and burn the scroll with the prophecy that the lesser magistrates *"were not afraid, nor did they tear their garments."*[76] They thought only of their own self-preservation, rather than to do what was right and necessary. They failed to "stand in the gap."[77] The king then orders the arrest of Baruch and Jeremiah.

Knox rightly castigates the princes of Judah and points out to the nobles of Scotland the results, namely, increased judgment not only upon the king's family, *but upon the whole nation:*

> I will punish him, his family, and his servants for their iniquity; and I will bring on them, *on the inhabitants of Jerusalem, and on the men of Judah* all the doom that I have pronounced against them, but they did not heed.[78]

Knox not only wanted the nobles (lesser magistrates) of Scotland to see that they had a duty before God to act against unjust laws or edicts in their nation, but that their *failure to act* would affect the whole nation. And so it is with any lesser magistrate in any nation down through history – and in the future.

---

74 Jeremiah 36:16

75 Jeremiah 36:22-23

76 Jeremiah 36:24

77 Ezekiel 22:30-31

78 Jeremiah 36:31

In his Appellation, Knox takes to task those lesser magistrates who use the higher magistrate as an *excuse* for their inaction. He says to the nobles of Scotland as lesser magistrates:

> Shall you be excused, if with silence you pass over his iniquity? Be not deceived my lords. You are placed in authority for another purpose than to flatter your king in his folly and blind rage.[79]

He later exhorts them saying:

> Only at this time I thought it expedient to admonish you, that before God it shall not excuse you to allege, "We are no kings, and therefore neither can we reform religion, nor yet defend the persecuted."[80]

Finally, Knox states disdainfully, *"For now the common song of all men is, 'We must obey our kings, be they good or be they bad; for God has so commanded.'"*[81]

And so it is no different in our own day. Lesser magistrates have little to no appreciation for their own authority as magistrates, nor do they understand their grave duty in the sight of God to interpose against bad law made by higher magistrates. They often hide behind the excuse - "it is the law of the land."

Recently, I was at a school board meeting where many had gathered to oppose bad policy that the elected school board was implementing in the schools. The board was imposing the acceptance of homosexuality upon the students. They played the common song, telling us all that their hands were tied – they were just following state law (which was just following Federal law) and were powerless to do other than what they were commanded and expected to do.

This is false. They actually had a duty to stand against the bad law and refuse to implement it; to interpose on behalf of the students and the parents whose children would be corrupted by this bad policy. But they showed no fear of God; no concern for those parents or their children;

79 Knox, *Selected Writings*, 504-505.

80 Knox, *Selected Writings*, 508.

81 Knox, *Selected Writings*, 508.

rather, they hid behind the common song of "We are not kings - we must simply obey whether it be good or bad. Take it up with those who made the law." They should have interposed. They had a God-given duty and right to interpose.

Scripture illustrates repeatedly that God is pleased with the lesser magistrate who acts against unjust or immoral law, who *refuses* to sing the common song.

As an example of this, Knox cites the account of Ebed-Melech in Jeremiah 38:7-13. Jeremiah was in the dungeon being held prisoner on a false charge of treason. Ebed-Melech was a lesser magistrate in King Zedekiah's house. He informs the king of Jeremiah's mistreatment and interposes on Jeremiah's behalf by saying:

> My lord the king, these men [who put Jeremiah in the dungeon] have done evil in all they have done to Jeremiah the prophet, whom they have cast into the dungeon, and he is likely to die of hunger in the place where he is. For there is no more bread in the city.[82]

King Zedekiah upon hearing Ebed-Melech's interposition, orders this lesser magistrate to take thirty men and remove Jeremiah from the dungeon.

Ebed-Melech acted righteously even though all other lesser magistrates either wanted Jeremiah dead or stood by in silence, concerned only for their own well-being.

The Lord tells Jeremiah that after Jerusalem falls and he is released from prison, he is to go and speak to Ebed-Melech the Ethiopian, saying:

> Thus says the Lord of hosts, the God of Israel: Behold, I will bring my words upon this city for adversity and not for good, and they shall be performed in that day before you. *But I will deliver you in that day*, says the Lord, and you shall not be given into the hand of the men of whom you are afraid. *For I will surely deliver you, and you shall not fall by the sword; but*

82 Jeremiah 38:9

> *your life shall be as a prize to you, because you have put your trust in Me,* says the Lord.[83]

Yes, God rewards lesser magistrates who will stand in the gap in defiance of oppression and tyranny – who will interpose even to their own hurt for the sake of others, and for the sake of truth.

83 Jeremiah 39:15-18

your life shall be as a prize to you, because you have put your trust in Me, says the Lord."

God, [illegible] lesser magistrates who will stand in the gap [illegible] of oppression and tyranny — who will interpose even their own [illegible] for the sake of others, and for the sake of truth.

# When Lesser Magistrates Go Rogue

# Chapter 9

In February of 2004, America heard tell of a bold lesser magistrate who was willing to oppose the higher magistrate. The only problem was – *he was wicked.*

Gavin Newsom, the mayor of San Francisco, decided to defy state law and issue state marriage licenses to homosexuals. In just one week, over six thousand sodomites obtained the licenses, including many who traveled to San Francisco from over 20 different states (in an attempt to export their filth all across the nation). God defines such "relationships" as criminal[84] and "lawless."[85] Scripture resolutely condemns such behavior.[86]

Gavin Newsom is the quintessential example of a lesser magistrate gone rogue. For an entire week, state and federal officials stood by and did nothing, nor was there any opposition on the part of Christians out on the streets while Newsom and city officials continued to spit upon the law of God.

Finally, a group of fourteen young Christian men and women stepped forward on February 19, 2004, one week into the immoral and unlawful "marriages." They had enough of this impugning of God's law going unanswered. The ten men brushed their way past a security officer, and went straight to the head of the line of hundreds of homosexuals waiting to "marry." They positioned themselves in the doorway to blockade it, and boldly announced *"Okay folks, the show is over!"*[87]

This of course caused no small stir. Pushing and shoving ensued, but the young men held their positions. They declared God's law and great salvation,

---

84 Leviticus 20:13

85 2 Peter 2:6-8

86 Genesis 19:1-11; Leviticus 18:22; Judges 19:16-24; I Kings 15:11-12; Romans 1:18-32; I Corinthians 6:9; I Timothy 1:9-10; Jude 7.

87 Matthew Trewhella, *A Time For War: Why Ten Young Men Stormed the Gates of Hell in San Francisco*, Feb.20, 2004.Web. < http://www.mercyseat.net/TenMenStormed.html>.

and sang hymns while the homosexuals wailed and police and sheriff's deputies assembled to put the men in compliance holds and drag them away. This action was caught by news media - local, national, and international. The four young women filmed and photographed the incident.

Eight of the men were dragged through the building and thrown out a side door. The other two were taken to jail and charged with trespassing. What mattered however was - *a godly standard had been raised in San Francisco around which men could rally.*

Gavin Newsom, the unjust lesser magistrate, was about to see his little parade for perversion come crashing down around him. The very next day, California Governor Arnold Schwarzenegger, the higher magistrate, who had been silent about these "marriages" the entire first week, broke his silence and declared that these marriages *must stop*. He pointed to the actions of the young Christians the day before as his motivating reason for finally speaking out.[88]

Yes, lesser magistrates, just like superior magistrates, can act unjustly. When they do, it is the duty of the higher magistrate, equal fellow magistrates, or even a subordinate to the unjust magistrate, to interpose and rein in that lesser magistrate. Superior magistrates, equal magistrates, and subordinates of the lesser magistrate - have a right and duty to oppose and act against the unjust actions of lesser magistrates.

Knox, in his Appellation, speaks of rogue actions by lesser magistrates. He cites Jeremiah chapters 37-38 as an example. In this passage, Jeremiah was arrested for treason because he *wasn't* cheering on the war effort against the Babylonians with pom-poms in hand. In fact, the Lord was having him prophecy that Jerusalem was going to fall to the Babylonians. He was preaching surrender. For this, he was arrested for treason.

Concerning this, Knox points out in his *A Godly Letter of Warning (1553):*

> Let a thing here be noted, that the prophet of God sometimes may teach treason against kings, and yet neither he nor such as obey the word, spoken in the Lord's name by him, offend God.[89]

---

88 Edward Epstein, San Francisco Chronicle, *Governor fears unrest unless same-sex marriages are halted.* Feb.23, 2004. Web. <http://www.sfgate.com/cgibin/article.cgi?f=/c/a/2004/02/23/MNGJ7566RL1.DTL>.

89 Knox, *Selected Writings,* 165-166.

Jeremiah was arrested by a lesser magistrate, the captain of the guard, one Irijah. There are always those who are *too* anxious to serve the State. Irijah was one of those kinds of people. Irijah handed Jeremiah over to the princes of Judah, lesser magistrates themselves (though higher than Irijah). They were angry at Jeremiah, struck him, and threw him into the dungeon.

King Zedekiah then hears that Jeremiah has been captured. He meets with Jeremiah secretly to ask, "Is there any word from the Lord?" Jeremiah bluntly tells the king "There is. You shall be delivered into the hand of the king of Babylon."[90] Not quite what Zedekiah had hoped to hear.

Jeremiah then appeals to the king, *as the higher or chief magistrate,* regarding his mistreatment at the hands of the lesser magistrates, namely the princes. As a result of his plea, Zedekiah has Jeremiah removed from the dungeon to the prison court – a marked improvement in conditions.

But the story is not over. The lesser magistrates – the princes – hear of this and they appeal to King Zedekiah to put Jeremiah to death! The king replies "Look, he is in your hand. For the king can do nothing against you."[91] Just as the lesser magistrates hide behind the saying "*We're just following the law; there's nothing we can do; it's the law of the land*" when evil or injustice is codified into law by higher magistrates, so also, too often when a lesser magistrate goes rogue and acts unjustly, we hear the higher magistrate make excuses for not intervening (or they do what Governor Schwarzenegger first did and remain strangely silent).

After Zedekiah's act of weakness, Jeremiah is taken by the lesser magistrates and placed back into the dungeon itself.

But the story is still not over. As noted in the last chapter, one lone lesser magistrate, Ebed-Melech, an Ethiopian, learns of Jeremiah's condition and appeals to Zedekiah on his behalf. Zedekiah responds positively to this lesser magistrate's words, and orders Ebed-Melech to take thirty men and lift Jeremiah up out of the dungeon.[92]

What we learn from all of this is that both the higher magistrate and other lesser magistrates have a duty and right to act against the unjust actions of lesser magistrates. When a lesser magistrate goes rogue and plays the oppressor and tyrant, or imposes unjust law, the higher mag-

90 Jeremiah 37:17

91 Jeremiah 38:4-5

92 Jeremiah 37:7-11

istrate and other lesser magistrates must clearly interpose and take him to task.

In the end, God rewarded Ebed-Melech for his just actions as a lesser magistrate.[93] But notice the end of those princes who acted unjustly in their office as lesser magistrates. The Scripture says that Nebuchadnezzar, king of Babylon, *"killed all the nobles of Judah."*[94]

When tyranny presents itself, almost never do all the lesser magistrates stand and resist, whether the oppression and tyranny comes from the higher magistrate or from other lesser magistrates. Even when some lesser magistrates take a stand, usually the majority will go along with the tyranny. This is how things always go when good becomes evil and evil becomes good in a nation. *Most go along to get along.* That's what sustained Hitler's Germany and Stalin's Russia.

The people's hope is that lesser magistrates everywhere will understand their God-given right and duty to interpose - stand in the gap - when oppression and tyranny raises its ugly head. The people must then rally around those lesser magistrates who actually do stand.

---

93 Jeremiah 39:15-18

94 Jeremiah 39:6

# The Response of the Tyrannical Higher Magistrate

# Chapter 10

Higher magistrates tend to respond negatively when their orders, laws, or edicts are defied. They don't take kindly to disobedience. A short perusal of history makes that fact glaringly clear.

You may recall Emperor Caligula did not respond appreciatively to Governor Petronius when the governor refused to uphold the law to place a statue of Caligula in the temple. Caligula was outraged. He ordered Petronius to kill himself.

The emperor told the governor, "I will make you an example to the present and to all future ages that they may not dare to contradict the commands of their emperor."[95]

When Moses told Pharaoh to "let My people go," Pharaoh did not respond by saying "Oh, sure." Rather, he ordered the Israelites to make bricks without straw.[96]

Things often get worse before they get better when a stand is made against tyranny or unjust/immoral laws or policies. *There will be a fight.* The veneer of "civility" will dissipate.

King Charles I of England didn't go quietly into the night because Parliament challenged his belief in the divine right of kings.

King George didn't change his mind, bring his troops home, and get with the program just because the American colonists issued a Declaration of Independence.

Higher magistrates like being obeyed. When someone stands against their tyranny or unjust/immmoral law, they do not meekly acquiesce. They will fight to have the lesser magistrates and people conform. The United States Federal government is no different.

95 Josephus, *Works,* 85-89.

96 Exodus 5:6-10

Higher magistrates committed to unjust or immoral law will always demonize, marginalize, undermine, and criminalize any lesser magistrate who takes a stand to oppose their bad law. We should not be surprised when our Federal government rejects the interposition of a lesser magistrate in America, anymore than when Emperor Caligula rejected the interposition of Governor Petronius. Higher magistrates bent on tyranny never want to recognize the legitimate authority of lesser magistrates when they are busy making unjust/immoral laws or orders, as our Federal government is doing in our day.

The vast majority of lesser magistrates will compromise moral character in order to avoid conflict, thinking mostly of their own self interests. They will not defy the higher magistrate. Some may make a squabble, but will conform once the Federal courts rule against them. Present-day American jurisprudence wants us to believe that the Federal courts take precedent over all others and we should *ipso facto* accept their rulings.

Other lesser magistrates will refuse to resist because of concern for their own safety. When the lesser magistrate acts in defiance of the superior authority, he – as Suetonius said – *"grabs the wolf by the ears."* By that, he meant, on the one hand he has to consider the justice needed, and on the other hand he must contemplate self-preservation.

When that rare magistrate or magistrates take a stand, not only will the higher authority attack the lesser magistrate who resists, but other self-serving lesser magistrates will also attack such a magistrate. Those who support the unjust or immoral law will revile the one who resists for not following the "law of the land."

The myriad of immoral rulings made by the U.S. Supreme Court, and bad laws made by the Federal government, including legalizing the killing of the preborn and decriminalizing sodomy, are attacks upon the rule of law in our nation. To think that we should just stand by while innocent babies die, or submit to our children being taught that sodomy is moral, under the guise of "we must respect the rule of law" while such deeds are being done – *actually stands the rule of law on its head.*

We have no reason or obligation to obey the State when they *redefine* the rule of law contrary to divine law, and create law which is antithetical to the justice God has declared to apply to all men. Rather, men have a duty to resist and oppose unjust or immoral law.

The political class in the United States (those who are a part of government or who personally benefit from their patronage system) live like kings, especially those within the Federal government. They have been learning to view themselves as an aristocracy, and this leads them to view the people as peasants for their disposal. The government has been pillaging the private sector for their own aggrandizement. They seize money via taxation through the coercive arm of the State, and then use that money to forge chains to bind the people to the State, and make them dependent upon it.

The lesser magistrates and the people must understand that when they interpose against unjust law, there will be a fight. Their reputation will be maligned, and they could end up imprisoned or abused in some fashion. Governing officials who resist need to understand that they act *not* for glory or political ambition - rather they do so because it is the right thing to do in the sight of God. The interposition of the lesser magistrates abates the just judgment of God on nations that have impugned His law.[97]

America's Federal government has become like an unleashed wild dog. The lesser magistrates who interpose on behalf of the people and in defiance of the tyranny of this Federal beast will need to have the fortitude and character of those lesser magistrates from Scotland long ago.

In Scotland, on April 6, 1320, eight earls and over forty nobles fixed their seals to what became known as the *Declaration of Arbroath*. These earls and nobles were the lesser magistrates of their day. They wrote their Declaration in opposition to the tyranny of Edward II, king of England. They stated in part:

> For so long as a hundred of us are left alive, we will yield in no least way to English rule. It is in truth not for glory, nor for wealth, nor honours, but only and alone we fight for freedom ...which no good man surrenders, but with his life.[98]

97 Ezekiel 22:27-31

98 The Declaration of Arbroath. Apr. 6, 1320 AD. Web. <http://www.nas.gov.uk/about/090401.asp>

# The Role of the People

# Chapter 11

Remonstrance is an archaic word rarely used today. But it is exactly what the people are supposed to do in order to fulfill their role in combating tyranny. To remonstrate means to present strong arguments against an act, measure, or any course of proceedings.

Webster goes on to say that this can be done in public or private. He says, "When addressed to a public body, a prince or magistrate, it may be accompanied with a petition or supplication for the removal or prevention of some evil."[99]

Remonstrance by the people played an important role in the story of Petronius and Caligula. When Petronius decided to winter in Ptolemais before marching on Jerusalem the next spring, the Jews seized the opportunity to come and remonstrate before him.

Josephus tells us that tens of thousands of Jews – men, women and children – came to Ptolemais to petition Governor Petronius not to erect the statue of Caligula in the Temple. They informed him that they would die first, rather than accommodate themselves to such an egregious violation of God's law.[100]

Petronius became angry with the people (as all lesser magistrates tend to do, desiring the absence of conflict) and stated:

> If indeed I myself were emperor, and were at liberty to follow my own inclination, and then had designed to act thus, these your words would be justly spoken to me; but now Caesar has sent to me, I am under the necessity of being subservient to his decrees, because a disobedience to them will bring inevitable destruction.

99 Noah Webster, *American Dictionary of the English Language* (San Francisco, CA: Foundation for American Christian Education, 1828/1967)

100 Josephus, *Works*, 85-89.

Petronius remained resolute and continued intent on obeying Caligula's law and order. The Jews petitioned further, however. They ended by stating:

> If we should submit to you, we should be greatly reproached for our cowardice, as thereby showing ourselves ready to transgress our law; and we should incur the great anger of God also, who, even thyself being judge, is superior to Caligula.

Petronius again rebuffed them, but he was so moved by their pleas and the sight of tens of thousands of Jews remonstrating before him, that he removed himself to the city of Tiberius to further consider what he should do. Petronius hesitated; he did not take action to erect the statue, nor march towards the Temple.

Tens of thousands of Jews then followed Petronius to Tiberius. They again protested the evil of having the statue being placed in their Temple. They informed him that they were in no position to war against Rome, and then powerfully demonstrated the passion of their opposition by lying on the ground, and baring their necks before Petronius, offering for him to kill them there, saying, "We will die before we see our laws transgressed."

The Jews remained in Tiberius for forty days remonstrating before Petronius.

The Jews also sent a delegation of principal men, including Aristobulus, the brother of King Agrippa, to meet with Petronius privately. They pointed to the resolve of the people and asked Petronius to write to Caligula to rescind his law to install the statue.

Petronius took time to think matters over after the Jews had departed. He later called them back to Tiberius.

When they arrived, Petronius had assembled two legions of soldiers – 12,000 men. The soldiers stood on one side, and the Jews lined up opposite of them. The Jews did not know if they would all be killed, as they had bared their necks to the ground their last visit. Petronius restated the law issued by Caligula. He went on to inform them that Caligula's "wrath would, without delay, be executed on such as had the courage to disobey what he had commanded, and that immediately."

Petronius then stepped between the soldiers and the Jews and made his famous speech, wherein he made known his act of interposition[101] on behalf of the Jews as a lesser magistrate.

He concluded his speech by saying:

> ...and may God be your assistant, for His authority is beyond all the contrivance and power of men; and may He procure you the preservation of your ancient laws, and may not He be deprived, though without your consent, of His accustomed honors. But if Caligula be irritated, and turn the violence of his rage upon me, I will rather undergo all the danger and affliction that may come either on my body or my soul, than see so many of you perish, while you are acting in so excellent a manner. Therefore, every one of you, go your way about your own occupations, and fall to the cultivation of your ground; I will myself send to Rome, and will not refuse to serve you in all things, both by myself and by my friends.[102]

The impact the people had upon Governor Petronius is evident. *Notice that tens of thousands remonstrated before him.* The people have a duty to protest unjust or immoral law.

The role of the people in applying the lesser magistrate doctrine is to remonstrate before the lesser magistrate, and rally behind him when he takes a stand. The lesser magistrates often will not act until the people plead their case, and the magistrates are assured of their support.

It was the people themselves who interposed on behalf of Pastor Tokes in Romania. After the people took action, many lesser magistrates joined in the revolution, refusing to obey Ceausescu's orders.

When the people do not understand the importance of their role in seeing the lesser magistrate doctrine exercised, or believe the common song that they are to have unlimited obedience to the civil government, the results are disastrous.

An example of how things turn out badly when the people *fail* to rally behind the lesser magistrate is seen in what happened to Judge Roy

101 See Chapter 2 on Interposition.

102 Josephus, *Works*, 85-89.

Moore, the Chief Justice of the Alabama Supreme Court. In August of 2001, Judge Moore had a monument of the Ten Commandments placed in the rotunda of the state judicial building. The American Civil Liberties Union (ACLU) immediately decried Judge Moore's actions by stating, "Our courts should enforce secular law, not God's law."[103]

Moore was assailed by the Federal government through their courts. They condemned his actions, and ordered the Ten Commandments removed from the building.

The people did *not* rally behind Judge Moore who was clearly committing an act of interposition as a lesser magistrate. Rather, most of the people, so inculcated with years of statist dogma through the education system and American media, believed the courts have the final say and they had to simply conform and accommodate to whatever the Federal courts dictate. They sat by in silence, or actually condemned Judge Moore. Many Christian leaders, steeped in their false teaching that Christians must always obey the government, abandoned Moore or spoke against him.

In the end, Chief Justice Moore's own fellow justices on the Alabama Supreme Court turned against him, as did countless other lesser magistrates. He was ordered to pay hundreds of thousands of dollars to atheistic attorneys, and was removed from office. The U.S. President at the time, George W. Bush, shamefully honored Moore's greatest antagonist, Alabama Attorney General Bill Pryor, with a Federal judgeship.

Judge Moore was defeated in his effort to point to God's law as the foundation of law in the State of Alabama (and all of Western Civilization) because the people failed miserably to rally behind a courageous lesser magistrate.

It is important to note that the lesser magistrate does *not* need the majority of the people to support him before he can act. Some of the most important and necessary actions down through history were done without a majority. In fact, human nature is such that the majority usually only have an interest in their own well-being and livelihoods.

In truth, the lesser magistrate does not need *any* support from the people in order to act. He can and should act when warranted because

103 *Alabama Chief Justice Unveils Ten Commandments in State Supreme Court.* Associated Press. Aug.1, 2001. Web. <http://www.foxnews.com/story/0,2933,31137,00.html>

he has the right and duty in the sight of God to do so. Nevertheless, the people should (and do) - *by their action or inaction* - play a role of immense importance when it comes to the effectiveness of the lesser magistrates' interposition against tyranny.

# The Lesser Magistrate Doctrine in Our Day

# Chapter 12

The lesser magistrate doctrine isn't just some ancient teaching that we can study, but which is void of any practical application in our own day. The nature of man does not change. The need for lesser magistrates to interpose raises its head from time to time in the course of human events.

Have you been to Washington, D.C. lately? It is a veritable fortress. The Federal government has made it such not only because they are concerned about threats from without; their greater concern has been threats from *within*. The fortress-like nature of the place reminds one of what Plato said to the tyrant Dionysius when he saw him on the streets of Sicily surrounded by his many bodyguards – "What harm have you done that you should need to have so many guards?"[104]

The Federal government has harmed the American people. Review their laws, policies, and bureaucracies, and you see that they have caused *much harm* to the institutions and traditions of our people. The Federal government has already attacked and abridged liberty. They are now in the process of plundering the American people.

The Christian author C.S. Lewis spoke of a tyranny where the State tries to make the citizens dependent upon it, through which they slowly enslave the people. He wrote:

> Of all tyrannies, a tyranny sincerely exercised for the good of its victims may be the most oppressive. It would be better to live under robber barons than under omnipotent moral busybodies. The robber baron's cruelty may sometimes sleep, his cupidity may at some point be satiated; but those who torment

104 Salisbury, *Policraticus*, 17.

> us for our own good will torment us without end for they do so with the approval of their own conscience.[105]

The Federal government has been doing this to the American people for decades. Through such actions of "benevolence," Americans are now nearly a completely conquered people. They no longer cherish freedom or liberty. Many Americans already expect and desire the government to wipe their rear ends and blow their noses from the cradle to the grave. The Federal government seizes money from the people through taxation and then uses the money to forge the people's chains and make them dependent upon the State.

We saw an example of this in the not too distant past. After the Obama administration strong-armed their so-called Affordable Health Care Reform Act through Congress, they immediately sent out their representatives to convince the American people of *"how this will benefit them."*

Yet, the legislation is an attack on freedom. It demonstrates another action taken by the Federal government to push well beyond the boundaries of proper government. From a biblical and Constitutional point of view, these new laws are not legitimate to the purpose of good or lawful government. They bind people to the State and make them dependent upon it.

The lesser magistrates have the right and duty to interpose against law and policy that violates the Constitution (regardless of how the U.S. Supreme Court defines violations), and/or that attacks the person, property, or liberty of those within their jurisdiction of authority, and/or that impugns the law of God.

While preparing this book, several examples of lesser magistrates taking action of interposition have been highlighted in the press – in plain sight for all to see. President Barack Obama's Affordable Health Care Reform Act was challenged by 27 states.[106] Six states have enacted legislation which defies it altogether.[107] These State Attorneys General and legislators serve as lesser magistrates, interposing not only to defend

---

105 C.S. Lewis, *God in the Dock* (Grand Rapids, MI: Eerdmans Publishing Company, 1970) 292.

106 Brandon Stewart. *List of 27 States Suing Over Obamacare.* The Foundry. 17 Jan. 2011. Web. <http://blog.heritage.org/2011/01/17/list-of-states-suing-over-obamacare/>

107 Mike Maharrey. *Six states defy feds.* Tenth Amendment Center. 7 Nov. 2012. Web. <http://tenthamendmentcenter.com/2012/11/07/national-press-release-six-states-defy-feds/>

the liberty of the people under their jurisdictions, but also protecting their very persons against the tyranny of the higher authority.

Arizona and other states have taken action to defend their borders against illegal immigration. This has resulted in fights with a Federal government who appears more concerned about granting greater freedoms to illegal foreigners than to its own citizens.[108]

A number of other states have defunded Planned Parenthood of all tax dollars, including Indiana and Texas. This has resulted in a drawn out fight with the Federal government as it insists on giving this bloodthirsty organization (and others in the population control industry) hundreds of millions of our tax dollars each year.[109]

We also see the doctrine demonstrated by lesser magistrates regarding the Second Amendment of the U.S. Constitution. Eight states have passed Firearms Freedom Act legislation.[110] This legislation interposes against bad Federal law and policy which undermines the right of Americans to keep and bear arms. News articles about lesser magistrates, both collectively and individually, taking a stand over this matter, are readily found in the press.[111]

On a state level, the Attorney General of Illinois ordered the Illinois State Police in that state to make public the names of gun owners. Officials of that agency (lesser magistrates) refused to do so, resulting in ongoing legislative and court fights between the lesser and higher authority.[112]

The question that remains to be seen in these events and many others is – will the lesser magistrates merely squabble with the Federal

108 Alia Beard Rau. *Arizona to defend its tough immigration law at Supreme Court.* USA Today. 21 Apr. 2012. Web. <http://www.usatoday.com/news/washington/judicial/story/2012-04-21/arizona-immigration-law-sb-1070/54462022/1>

109 Judy Keen. *State lawmakers work to defund Planned Parenthood.* USA Today. 26 May 2011. Web. <http://www.usatoday.com/news/nation/2011-05-25-Planned-Parenthood-funding-abortion-opponents_n.htm>

110 *Firearms Freedom Act.* Lew Rockwell. Web. <http://www.lewrockwell.com/rep3/firearms-freedom-act.html#mt> <http://firearmsfreedomact.com/>

111 *Wyoming legislators prepare to defy a Federal gun ban.* IRNUSA News.10 Jan. 2013 Web. < http://www.irnnews.com/2013/01/10/wyoming-legislators-prepare-to-defy-a-federal-gun-ban/> Also: Todd Starnes. *Wyoming Considers Gun Protection Bill.* Fox News. 11 Jan. 2013. Web. < http://radio.foxnews.com/toddstarnes/top-stories/wyoming-considers-gun-freedom-bill.html> Also: David Adamsinky. *Kentucky sheriff to defy any Obama gun grab.* Red State. 11 Jan. 2013. Web. <http://www.redstate.com/davidadamsinky/2013/01/10/kentucky-sheriff-to-defy-any-obama-gun-grab/> Also: *Sheriff says he'll undermine gun ban.* The Gazette. 23 Feb. 2010. Web. < http://www.gazette.com/opinion/state-94668-gun-ban.html>

112 Judson Berger. *Illinois Officials Spar Over Order to Make List of Gun Owners Public.* Fox News. 2 Mar. 2011. Web. <http://www.foxnews.com/politics/2011/03/02/illinois-officials-spar-order-make-list-gun-owners-public/>

government or higher authority over these matters, *or will they stand resolute in opposition to their abuse of power?*

The standard operating procedure in the past has been that the lesser magistrates put up a fuss regarding tyranny, but only until a Federal court rules the tyranny to be "legal." Then the lesser magistrates comply.

Those of a more jaded stripe may even view such actions by lesser magistrates as being politically motivated. The lower magistrates know that the people do not like a Federal law or policy, so they put up a fight, but then do nothing else to resist once a Federal court rules against them. They then sing the common song of which Knox spoke: "We must obey our kings, be they good or be they bad; for God has so commanded."[113]

Lesser magistrates today need to understand that state governments were not intended to be mere *conduits* for enacting Federal public policies. They are not to be mere implementation centers through which the Federal government dispenses its unjust policies, decisions, and laws

The interposition of the lesser magistrates is absolutely critical for the preservation of liberty. The hour for them to stand is upon us. We have a Federal government that is now trampling our cherished liberties, and assaulting our persons and property. It has caused much harm to the Christian institutions and traditions of our people. They are steeped in governmental mischief. They have foisted upon us endless regulations and debilitating lawsuits. They seem to be at war with much of the American people. They appear clearly intent upon scrubbing the nation of any Christian influence.

The Bible says "If anyone will not work, neither shall he eat,"[114] so this government creates a society where you don't have to work and you still get to eat. The Bible says marriage is between a man and a woman,[115] so this government wants to make it between a man and man or a woman and a woman. The Bible says the firstfruit of our increase is to go to the Lord,[116] so this government takes the firstfruit right out of American's paychecks before they can give it to the Lord. The Bible says, "You shall not commit adultery", so this government says that adultery is no crime at all. And on and on.

113 Knox, *Selected Writings*, 508.

114 2 Thessalonians 3:10

115 Mark 10:6-8

116 Proverbs 3:9

The interposition of the lesser magistrate is also critically important for the protection of life. This is paramount. The Founders of our nation, when they penned the Declaration of Independence, declared "Life" itself to be the first right people are endowed with by their Creator. Abortion is the medically disguised murder of a helpless preborn child. Abortion is a clear violation of God's law. The Scripture declares *"You shall not murder."*[117]

The U.S. Supreme Court ruling in Roe v. Wade, as well as its companion case, Doe v. Bolton, represent unjust and immoral rulings because they contravene the law of God. On this matter, the lesser magistrates are clearly obligated to resist and actively oppose the Federal government.

Of all of the tyranny and injustice perpetrated by our nation's Federal government, abortion is the worst because it involves the actual killing of an innocent person. The lesser magistrates should have taken a stand *immediately* back in 1973 when the Federal government made the preborn open game to those who kill for profit. Yet, forty years later, the brutal killings continue.

When will a state stand in defiance of Federal tyranny? And if lesser magistrates will not stand over this matter – a group of innocent people being adjudicated to be openly killed by another group of people - then what cause will they stand on, and when?

Presently, not only is the law of God being contravened regarding murder of the innocent, but also regarding sodomy.[118] The Federal government decriminalized it in 2003.[119] The Federal beast has since busied itself with a plethora of public policy changes to expand its homosexualization of America.

The Federal government has been incessant in shoving the filth of sodomy upon Americans. This impugning of the law of God has reached the point where God's created order regarding marriage is threatened.

Some lesser magistrates recognize the threat and *have* taken action against these immoral laws and policies. As of 2013, thirty-one states have enacted constitutional amendments to their state constitutions in order to assure that marriage conforms to the law and created order of

117 Exodus 20:10

118 Leviticus 20:13; Romans 1:18-32; I Corinthians 6:9-11; Jude 7

119 Lawrence v. Texas, 539 U.S. 558 (2003)

God by declaring that marriage is between a man and a woman only. *But will they continue to stand when the U.S. Supreme Court rules otherwise?*

In the Magdeburg Confession, while discussing the fourth and worst degree of tyranny, in a near prophetic statement regarding our own day here in America, the pastors stated the following:

> Therefore, if now the leader or Caesar proceeds to such height of insanity only in that of natural knowledge which governs the society of civil life and uprightness, *that he abolishes the law concerning marriages and chastity, and himself sets up a contrary law of roving unclean lusts,* to the effect that the wives and daughters of men are to be prostituted – in such a case, doubtless, no clear-thinking person would have any hesitation about the divine right and commandment that such a leader or monarch ought to be curbed by everyone in his most wicked attempt, even by the lowest of the lowest magistrates with whatever power they may have.[120]

To the pastors of Magdeburg, all magistrates possess delegated authority from God. Therefore, they have a right and duty to oppose the magistrate-turned-tyrant when he makes law contrary to the law and Word of God. Their Confession set forth a biblical and historical foundation which strengthened the consciences of the magistrates in Magdeburg to resist the unjust and immoral law of Emperor Charles V.

Only time will tell if America's lesser magistrates are just putting up a token fight against the perverting of marriage. Will they stand even when the Federal dog bites back and presses all to embrace it whether legislatively or judicially? Will they join the higher authority in their rebellion against God, or will they do their duty in the sight of God and resist? Even concerning state authority, when will a city council, or mayor, or county clerk refuse obedience when a state legislature "legalizes" homosexual marriage?

There comes a time when the lesser magistrates must move beyond mere squabbling with the higher authority. There comes a time when men must cross swords. The lesser magistrates provide the best opportunity

120 Colvin, *Magdeburg Confession*, 60.

for this to be accomplished bloodlessly, but history has proven there are times when they must redden their swords.

The nobles of England interposed against the tyranny of King John in 1215. They were the lesser magistrates of their day. The stand they took with their willingness to fight resulted in the defeat of tyranny. The freedoms and rights recognized on the field that day at Runnymede were enshrined in the Magna Carta, which has had impact on freedom-loving nations to this day. They did it all bloodlessly, but it was their resolve and combined swords – and willingness to use them - that convinced the tyrant authority to capitulate.

A recent example, of the lesser magistrates crossing swords with the higher authority is seen in what took place in Honduras.

On June 28, 2009, then Honduran President, Jose Zelaya, was seized and shipped off to Costa Rica by Honduran military personnel. This was not a "military coup" as the press reported, rather, this was the lawful action of lesser magistrates against a tyrant who wanted to usurp the Honduran Constitution for his own dictatorial designs.[121]

In Honduras, the Senate, the Congress, the Attorney General, and the Supreme Court all took action as lesser magistrates to resist the unjust orders of President Zelaya. The magistrates were able to put down the tyranny of the higher authority. They did it bloodlessly. And they did it through interposition.

Here's a brief summary of the facts leading up to President Zelaya's removal:

When President Zelaya initially took office, he swore, "I promise to be faithful to the Republic and to obey and make others obey the Constitution and the laws."[122]

Zelaya however, with his Council of Ministers (his Cabinet Council), produced the Executive Decree PCM-005-2009 in early 2009 which had the ultimate goal of summoning a National Constituent Assembly to make a new Constitution, which would allow the elimination of the "Articulos Petreos", an act that was unconstitutional and is considered as a crime of "Treason to the Country."

The Attorney General began a judicial action that ended with a decree prohibiting the consultation, as this was improper behavior by

---

121 Mary Anastasia O'Grady. *Why Honduras Sent Zelaya Away*. Wall Street Journal. 13, Jul. 2009. Web. <http://online.wsj.com/article/SB124744094880829815.html>

122 Art. 322 of Honduran Constitution

the Executive Power. The Attorney General publicly warned that the President's behavior and that of his advisors was illegal.

The President then, again with his Council of Ministers, emitted Executive Decree PCM-019-2009 which annulled the previous Executive Decree, and which ordered that a national referendum would take place on Sunday, June 28, 2009, in which the following question would be asked: "Are you in favor with the addition of a fourth voting box in the general elections of 2009, in which the people will decide on the summon of a National Constituent Assembly?"

The Honduran Supreme Court ruled that the referendum violated the Constitution. President Zelaya moved forward anyway, and on June 24th he fired military General Romeo Vasquez when he *refused* Zelaya's order to distribute ballots for the June 28th referendum. The Supreme Court ruled that Vasquez should be reinstated, but Zelaya would not do it, and proceeded with the illegal referendum.

The Supreme Electoral Tribunal and the General Attorney of State began legal actions to confiscate the referendum's material and named the Air Force Chief as depositary of the confiscated items.

The President and a mob of his followers however, broke the Order of Legality, rejected the resolution by the judiciary, and assaulted the Air Force facilities in Tegucigalpa where the confiscated materials were being kept. Zelaya misused his authority as President of Honduras; publicly expressed that he would not respect the rulings of the judicial power, and put forward that the legislative power was not representative of the people, but believed he spoke for the people as he had been elected president of Honduras.

A multi-party commission named by Congress to investigate the President concluded that Zelaya had violated Honduran law. That commission asked Congress to declare him unfit to govern and to begin a legal process of impeachment.

The Honduran Senate passed a resolution declaring that the President had violated the Constitution on eighteen counts. It petitioned the Honduran Supreme Court to issue an arrest order to stop Zelaya from continuing with the violations.

The Armed Forces of Honduras was directed to seize Zelaya, and re-establish order and legality. The National Congress then followed the constitutional process established in Article 242 of the Honduran

Constitution, regarding the succession of the President in case of a definite absence.

In conclusion, the Honduran lesser magistrates simply took action against Zelaya's tyranny, as they had a God-given duty to do. These lesser magistrates accomplished a bloodless resolution, even though the leftists, socialists, and statists did everything they could to cause bloodshed by their usual tactics of agitation, violence, masked faces, and intimidation.

Many of the socialist and typical one-world government leaders, including U.S. President Barack Obama, lined up *against* these lesser magistrates.[123] They threatened them with economic destruction in an attempt to get them to capitulate, and give up their sovereignty and freedom. They tried to make examples of them lest any other upstart nations get the idea to preserve their Constitution and liberty from tyrants.

Though the whole world of socialist leaders tried to ostracize them, these lesser magistrates were brave men who stood and did not waver. They deserve our respect and support. May they and the Honduran people who supported them be examples to us all.

In our arrogance, Americans often think they are above the political wrangling of some third-world country like Honduras, but as the rule of law crumbles in our country – people will increasingly see the need to take a stand against unbridled tyranny. The lesser magistrate doctrine provides the means whereby a proper and just stand can be made.

The American Church and the American people need to repent for having spurned the law of God. If we do not, we will one day see what a taskmaster the Statists or Islamists are, and rue the day we threw off His rule. If the lesser magistrates do not stand against the tyranny and injustice of this Federal beast, America is doomed.

123 *Obama says Honduras coup illegal.* BBC News. 29 Jun. 2009. Web. <http://news.bbc.co.uk/2/hi/8125292.stm>

# Appendix A

# An Examination of Romans 13

## Three Convincing Proofs that Romans 13 Does NOT Teach Unlimited Obedience to the Civil Government

This short article is written to give three convincing proofs that Romans 13 does *not* teach that we are to give unlimited obedience to the State as some Christian men teach. The three convincing proofs are:

1. Nowhere does Romans 13 state that we are to give unlimited obedience to the civil government, rather men impose such thoughts upon the text.
2. Proper hermeneutics forbids such a conclusion – that we are to have unlimited obedience to the civil government – because there are many passages of Scripture where the people of God *disobey* the civil government, and are commended by God for doing it.
3. Romans 13 contains limitation clauses that make it clear the civil government's authority is not unlimited, nor therefore, is our obedience to the civil government to be unlimited.

## The First Convincing Proof

First, nowhere does the Bible say that we are to have unlimited obedience to the civil government – *nowhere.* Yet, this *divine right of kings* – that whatever those in civil authority decree is to be obeyed - has been what various Christian men have asserted over the centuries. They base this idea on Romans 13:1-5. But where does Romans 13 teach unlimited obedience to the State? They *impose* that idea upon the text. The text itself reads:

> Let every soul be subject to the governing authorities. For there is no authority except from God, and the authorities that exist are appointed by God. [2] Therefore whoever resists the authority resists the ordinance of God, and those who resist will bring judgment on themselves. [3] For rulers are not a terror to good works, but to evil. Do you want to be unafraid of the authority? Do what is good, and you will have praise from the same. [4] For he is God's minister to you for good. But if you do evil, be afraid; for he does not bear the sword in vain; for he is God's minister, an avenger to execute wrath on him who practices evil. [5] Therefore you must be subject not only because of wrath but also for conscience' sake.

Yes, the text does say we are to be subject to the governing authorities, and that governments are established by God, but where does it say we are therefore to have unlimited obedience to the government? It does not. Again, they impose that upon the text.

In fact, there is *not one* scripture anywhere in all the Bible that demands or instructs unlimited obedience to the civil government. That fact, in and of itself, should suffice to convince that we are not to give unlimited obedience to the State, but we will continue to the second convincing proof.

## The Second Convincing Proof

The second convincing proof is that proper hermeneutics forbids such a conclusion – that we are to have unlimited obedience to the civil government – because there are many passages of Scripture where the people of God *disobey* the civil government, and are commended by God for doing it.

Good hermeneutics demands that we not read a verse or passage in a vacuum. The hallmark of good hermeneutics is "Scripture interprets scripture." In other words, every individual scripture (scripture with a small s) must be interpreted in light of the whole of God's Word (Scripture with a big S). "Scripture interprets scripture." We are to examine a particular verse in light of the whole of God's Word.

When we look at the whole of God's Word, we see that there are many passages which contradict the assertion that "we are to always obey the government." For example, Exodus 1:15-21 records the story of the Hebrew mid-wives who were commanded by the king to kill the male Hebrew babies. The Scripture says the mid-wives *"feared God,"*[124] and therefore refused to kill the male babies. God commended them for their actions, as the Scripture states, *"Therefore God dealt well with the midwives,* and the people multiplied and grew very mighty."[125]

The point is, if the assertion is true that God's people are *always* to obey the laws and orders of the government, this passage stands in complete contradiction to it.

In Daniel chapter six, we read that the king declared that no one could pray to any deity, but only to him.[126] Notice that this law was made in clear contradiction to the law of God. The men who conspired to make this law understood that the only charge they could raise against Daniel was one concerning "the law of his God."[127] Therefore they made a law according to man – "the law of the Medes and Persians."[128] This was a classic showdown where the law of man contravened – violated, opposed, and contradicted - the law and Word of God.

How should the people of God respond? Did Daniel obey this law? Did he say, "Oh, that is a bad law, but we must always obey the State?" No, Daniel took a brave and open stand in defiance of this unjust law. The Scripture says that "when Daniel knew that the writing was signed, he went home. And in his upper room, with his windows open towards

124 Exodus 1:21

125 Exodus 1:20

126 Daniel 6:7-9

127 Daniel 6:5

128 Daniel 6:8

Jerusalem, he knelt down on his knees three times that day, and prayed and gave thanks before his God."[129]

Notice he "knew" of the unjust law; his windows were "open" so all could see his non-compliance with the law; he "knelt down on his knees" so no one could mistake his defiance of the law; and, he did it "three times" in one day.

Again, if the assertion is true that God's people are always to obey the laws and orders of the State, this passage stands in complete contradiction to it.

The midwives were told *to do* something bad – kill the male babies – and they refused. Daniel was told *not* to do something good – pray to the Lord – and he refused. These two passages about the midwives and Daniel illustrate the standard the Church has followed historically, namely, when the State commands that which God forbids or forbids that which God commands, we have a duty to obey God rather than man.

The standard is that if a law enacted by the State contravenes the law or Word of God, we are to obey God, not the State.

Other passages also contradict the assertion that we are to always obey the State. For example, Hebrews 11:23 records how Moses' parents disobeyed the king. The Scripture reads, "By faith Moses, when he was born, was hidden three months by his parents, because they saw he was a beautiful child; *and they were not afraid of the king's command.*"[130] This is recorded in what Christians call the "Hall of Fame of Faith." Their actions are commended by the Word of God.

In Second Corinthians 11:32-33, Paul talks about how he avoided the government officials who were attempting to arrest him, by escaping down the side of the city wall. The Scripture reads, "In Damascus the governor, under Aretas the king, was guarding the city of Damascenes with a garrison, desiring to arrest me; *but I was let down in a basket through a window in the wall, and escaped from his hands.*"[131] Paul knew the government officials were trying to arrest him, but rather than submit, he craftily fled.

In the fifth chapter of Acts, the apostles were told by the authorities not to preach about Jesus. They refused to obey them and responded by

129 Daniel 6:10

130 Hebrews 11:23

131 2 Corinthians 11:32-33

saying, "*We ought rather to obey God than men.*"[132] When human authority contravenes the law or Word of God, we have a duty to obey God rather than man.

All these passages (and others) stand in complete contradiction to the idea that we are to *always* obey the government. If Romans 13 teaches that we are to have unlimited obedience to the State, these passage stand in contradiction to such an assertion.

So, nowhere in Romans 13 does it state that Christians are to have unlimited obedience to the civil government, and the hallmark rule of proper hermeneutics, "Scripture interprets scripture," repudiates such an assertion.

## The Third Convincing Proof

The third convincing proof that Romans 13 does not teach unlimited obedience to the civil government is that Romans 13 itself contains limitation clauses which limit the authority and function of the civil government, and therefore make clear that our obedience to the State is not to be unlimited.

The advocates of unlimited obedience to the State point to verse one which says, "Let every soul be subject to the governing authorities. For there is no authority except from God, and the authorities that exist are appointed by God," and verse five which says, "Therefore you must be subject, not only because of wrath but also for conscience' sake." They then impose upon the text that we are *always* to obey in *everything*, something which the text does not say.

The truth is, the passage *does* talk about obeying the authorities, *but there are conditions stated which limit the ruler's authority.* There are limitation clauses attached to what the Apostle Paul says in Romans 13. Verses three and four clearly limit the ruler's authority. The Scripture says:

> "For rulers are not a terror to good works, but to evil. Do you want to be unafraid of the authority? Do what is good, and you will have praise from the same. For he is God's minister to you for good. But if you do evil, be afraid: for he does not bear the sword in vain; for he is God's minister, an avenger to execute wrath on him who practices evil."

132 Acts 5:29

These are limitation clauses. The Scriptures are plain – the ruler's authority is not unlimited. He is to reward those who do good and punish those who do evil. *But what if he begins to punish those who do good, and reward those who do evil?* What if he makes law that rewards those who do evil, and law that punishes those who do good? Should he still be obeyed? As we saw previously, the Scriptures are clear – he should not be obeyed.

When the State commands that which God forbids or forbids that which God commands, we are to obey God rather than man. We are *not* to join the ruler in his rebellion against God. When he rules justly, we are not to resist him (v.2). But if he rules unjustly, then we are to resist him. In such instances, we are to obey God, rather than man.

God has established four governments in the earth, namely, self-government, family government, church government, and civil government. Each has its own function and jurisdiction in the lives of men. Family, church, and civil government assist in producing self-government in the individual.

Each of these governments has positions of authority. For instance, in family government, the man is the head; the wife is his helper in the governance of the home. In church government, positions include elders, pastors, and deacons. In civil government, positions range from the President to the policeman. The authority that each possesses is *delegated* authority – authority given to them of God.

The first verse of Romans 13 declares, "For there is no authority except from God, and the authorities that exist are appointed by God." Hence, the authority that the civil government possesses is delegated from God. The governing authority is, as verse 4 states, *"God's minister."* They are to therefore govern according to God's rule.

Most all would agree that when a father makes unjust or immoral laws or decrees in the home, that those under his jurisdiction are *not* bound to obey. Similarly, when a church officer governs unjustly within the church, neither should he be obeyed. But for some reason, when it comes to the civil government, men tend to think that the State can do most *anything* and they should always be obeyed.

Let us examine each of these three governments from Scripture.

Concerning family government, Colossians 3:20 states, "Children, *obey your parents in all things,* for this is well-pleasing to the Lord."

Notice this verse of Scripture says children are to obey *in all things.* There are *no* limitation clauses that limit the parent's authority, nor the extent of the child's obedience. Yet no one takes the parents authority as being limitless, nor the children needing to grant unlimited obedience.

All are agreed a father should not tell his child to go rob the corner gas station because if caught the child will face less severe punishment then he. Rather, the father has a duty before God to instruct the child in honesty and hard work, and to abhor theft. Hence, the father does not rule autonomously. He does not get to contravene the law of God just because he has a position of authority. The authority he has is *delegated* to him from God, and he has a duty therefore to govern his home in accordance with God's rule. So a child who is told by his father to go rob the corner gas station would be right *not* to obey his father.

Also, regarding church government, Hebrews 13:17 states, *"Obey those who rule over you, and be submissive,* for they watch out for your souls, as those who must give account. Let them do so with joy and not with grief, for that would be unprofitable for you."

Again, in this verse also there are *no* limitation clauses that limit the church officer's authority, nor the extent of a congregant's obedience. Yet no one takes their authority as being limitless, nor that those under them must give unlimited obedience.

Suppose a pastor was skimming out of the offering plate for his own personal gain and a congregant learned of it, but the pastor told him to not tell anyone so he could continue to steal. No one would think the congregant wrong for telling the elders anyway.

Yet, when it comes to civil government, some Christian leaders tell their people that they should *always* obey, even though there *are* limitation clauses when it comes to obedience to civil authorities. God's intent for rulers is that they be a terror not to good works, but to evil (v.3). They are to praise or reward those who do good (v.3). He is to be an avenger to execute wrath on him who practices evil (v.4). These are limitation clauses. This is God's definition of good government.

These limitation clauses clearly show the God-given role of the ruler or magistrate. When the civil authority governs according to God's intended function for his office, we are to "therefore," as the very next verse says, "be subject, not only because of wrath but also for conscience' sake" (v.5). When they do the opposite of what their delegated authority requires of them, however, we are *not* to obey them, as the passages under the second convincing proof revealed. We may have to actively resist them.[133]

The pastors of Magdeburg made an analogy between family government and civil government to make this very point:

> Let us take an example concerning a father of a family. If he should come to his wife or grown daughters in his house with some scoundrels in an obvious attempt to prostitute them, then they, his wife and daughters, not only would not render their husband and father the obedience which they otherwise owe him, but when they are not able to preserve their chastity in any other way, they would drive him off with stones.
>
> By the same argument, when the admission of Caesar into a magistrate's city brings with it a sure abolition of the true religion, the slaughter and exile of pious men – in this case, the defense of religion, of one's own life and the lives of other innocent persons (which defense the magistrate of that city owes to God and to the citizens by the commandment of God) removes another part of the obedience owed to Caesar, that he should not offer obedience by admitting Caesar into the city, according to the rule of Christ, because the duties owed, when they come with injury to God and others, and joined with sin, ought not to be paid to anyone, not even to a father or a magistrate.[134]

Romans 13 is clear that the civil magistrate is to mirror the justice and law of God in the earth. They are to reward those who do good and punish those who do evil. They are to execute wrath on those who practice evil. Therefore, when the magistrate makes or advocates law that is contrary to the law of God, the Christian has the duty to resist and oppose such law, and obey God rather than man.

Verse four makes clear that the authority the civil magistrate possesses is delegated authority. "For he is *God's minister* to you for good. But if you do

133 Exodus 1:15-21; Daniel 3; Daniel 6; Matthew 2:1-11; Acts 5:29

134 Matthew Colvin, trans., *The Magdeburg Confession (1550)* (North Charleston, SC: Createspace Publishing, 2012) 64.

evil, be afraid: for he does not bear the sword in vain; for he is *God's minister*, an avenger to execute wrath on him who practices evil." This concurs with verse one which makes clear the authority given to the ruler is given to him of God. Therefore he is to govern in accordance with God's rule.

God's law and Word is the standard for knowing what is good and what is evil. As the passage continues, verse nine of Romans 13 references the law of God. Why? Because it is the standard for knowing what is good and what is evil. It is the standard for both the public, as well as the personal lives of men. Paul is at that point in the passage moving from the public (the role of the magistrate) to the private. Both are in view. In other words, all men and all governments of men are accountable to the law and Word of God.

It stands to reason, if we are to *always* obey the State, regardless of what laws or orders the government makes or gives, then we, in effect, make the State *God*. The pastors of Magdeburg addressed this point in their Confession. They wrote:

> If God wanted superior magistrates who have become tyrants to be inviolable because of his ordinance and commandment, how many impious and absurd things would follow from this? Chiefly it would follow that God, by his own ordinance and command, is strengthening, nay, honoring and abetting evil works, and is hindering, nay, destroying good works; that there are contraries in the nature of God Himself, and in this ordinance by which He has instituted the magistrate; that God is no less against his own ordinance than he is for the human race.[135]

The idea that we are to always obey the civil government because it is appointed by God is absurd. The subjection they are due is not without limits. When they pervert their God-given role and function and begin to reward those who do evil and punish those who do good, rather than reward those who do good and punish those who do evil, *we have no duty to obey them*, rather, we have a duty to obey God. We must not join in the magistrate's rebellion against God, rather we must be true to the Lord. The Scriptures are clear on this.[136]

---

135 Colvin, *Magdeburg Confession*, 67.

136 Some mistakenly try to use First Peter 2:13-14 to try and further their teaching of unlimited obedience to the State. But the word translated "ordinance" in some translations is an old English word referring to

Christians are the best of citizens. We subject ourselves to the governing authorities and obey them in all points of civil law *except* in those points where they clearly contravene the law and Word of God. The pastors of Magdeburg declared this to Charles V in their Confession. The pastors wrote:

> As for other matters relating to your rule, we will gladly render obedience – as much as we are able and we owe you. The profession of our religion has diminished nothing from it; so that much true dignity and encouragement for the obedience owed rather flows from it for you. For we teach with the apostle Paul that you are the vicarious minister of God for promoting good works, and that obedience is owed to you in this role, just as to God, not only because of wrath or fear of your sword, but also because of conscience, that is, fear of the wrath and judgment of God.
>
> Although we cannot consider that all men equally comply with this doctrine, nor can we bring that about ourselves, nonetheless we can promise you this with the strength of a promise which is said about our ministry ("my word will not return to me void" Is. 55. Likewise, "Your labor will not be in vain in the Lord") that we will give from our Churches the greatest possible number of men who, if they be able to enjoy their own religion through you, will declare their obedience toward you in all owed and upright duties, and loyalty without hypocrisy, out of true love, not so much love of receiving fruit from you, as love of you yourself, perhaps more than all those whom you say are obedient to you, so that you mistakenly mark us for the crime of contumacy and rebellion.
>
> Although we are not able to look into the hearts of individuals, still, let us plainly affirm this about the city's general attitude

every "realm" or "institution" of human authority, not to every statute or law of man. As the verse goes on to say "whether to the king as supreme, or to governors, as to those who are sent by him for the punishment of evildoers and for the praise of those who do good." Hence, Peter is saying the same as Paul, and is not teaching unlimited obedience to the State.

> and will: that except for the preservation of our religion, nothing else is sought; that when this is gained, our Senate and citizens will be most obedient in all their proper duties according to your Majesty's laws.[137]

In this example, the pastors are making clear to Charles that they are his best citizens; that they obey in all areas, *except* where the law or Word of God is contravened.

Even when we disobey an unjust or immoral law, we benefit the ruler and the people of the nation as a whole. We benefit those in authority because, due to our disobedience, they are confronted with the reality of their rebellion against God. Our Christ-obeying disobedience gives them opportunity to recover themselves, and turn from their unjust and/or immoral deeds.

We benefit the people of the nation as a whole because we act as a check against tyranny. Our fealty is to Christ first, not to man, therefore when the State makes law that commands that which God forbids or forbids that which God commands, we obey God rather than man. This benefits the entire nation. The tyrant government is not allowed to continue unchecked in its tyranny. This is one way in which Christianity preserves liberty for a nation.

As Christians, we suffer at the hands of the State due to our disobedience of their unjust or immoral laws or decrees. The rest of the nation benefits from our suffering because we help rein in a tyrannical government. This has been the history of the Church. But the ungodly don't see it. They prefer select parts of history where Christian men affirmed the pagan doctrine of the divine right of kings by positing an unbiblical interpretation of Romans 13 and teaching unlimited obedience to the State.

Like Daniel said to Darius in Daniel 6:22 *"O king, I have committed no crime against you."* In other words, an unjust or immoral law is no law at all.

As Christian men and women, may we stand true to Christ, and to the law and Word of God.[138]

---

137 Colvin, *Magdeburg Confession,* 52.

138 For a list of common arguments against the lesser magistrate doctrine, including the Romans 13 assertion, and a response to each of them, read Christopher Goodman's *How Superior Powers Ought to be Obeyed by Their Subjects and Wherein They May Lawfully by God's Word be Disobeyed and Resisted* written in 1558. It is available at Kessinger Publishing, Kessinger.net.

## APPENDIX B

# THE LAWS OF A NATION SHOULD MIRROR THE LAW AND JUSTICE OF GOD

*"The commandment of the Lord is pure, enlightening the eyes."*

*Psalm 19:8*

Let us now examine the redemptive or mediatorial work of the law. When speaking of the redemptive work of the law, I do *not* mean that we are redeemed by the law. Men can only find redemption through Christ alone through faith in Him based upon His substitutionary, propitiatory work at Calvary on the cross.

What is meant by the redemptive work of the law is that the law plays *a part* in the redemptive process of man. We know this is so from the Scriptures. Galatians 3:24 for example, plainly states: *"Therefore the law was our tutor to bring us to Christ."* The moral law of God shows men they are sinners in need of Jesus for their Savior. This is the way in which the law of God plays a role in the redemptive process of man.

Romans 7:7-13 concurs with this:

> What shall we say then? Is the law sin? Certainly not! On the contrary, *I would not have known sin except through the law.* For I would not have known covetousness unless the law had said, "You shall not covet." [8] But sin, taking opportunity by the commandment, produced in me all manner of evil desire. For apart from the law sin was dead. [9] I was alive once without the law, but when the commandment came, sin revived and I died. [10] And the commandment, which was to bring life, I found to bring death. [11] For sin, taking occasion by the commandment, deceived me, and by it killed me. [12] Therefore the law is holy, and the commandment holy and just and good. [13] Has then what is good become death to me? Certainly not! But sin, that it might appear sin, was producing death in me through what is good, *so that sin through the commandment might become exceedingly sinful.*

Again, the law of God shows men they have sinned and are in need of a Savior. The law was given "that every mouth may be stopped and all the world may become guilty before God" (Romans 3:19-20). Hence, the law of God plays a critical role in the redemptive process of man – and that is what is meant regarding the redemptive work of the law.

Not only does the law of God play an important part regarding the very salvation of men's souls in what the Church declares to men, but also through the realms of family government and civil government. *Both of these realms are to also inform those under their respective jurisdictions when God's law has been violated.*

Family government and civil government are to *mirror* the law and justice of God. They are to mirror the law and justice of God in their rule. For example, we do this when we teach our children not to steal. We correct and punish them if they do steal. Thus, we are teaching them the law and justice of God. And so it is with the civil government. Those under their jurisdiction are told not to steal. They are punished if they do steal. In this way, civil government is mirroring the law and justice of God.

This too shows men they have violated God's law and are in need of redemption (which is found in Christ alone). Who is the law for? I Tim.1:9-10 states:

> [9]Knowing this: that the law is not made for a righteous person, but for the lawless and insubordinate, for the ungodly and for sinners, for the unholy and profane, for murderers of fathers and murderers of mothers, for manslayers, [10] for fornicators, for sodomites, for kidnappers, for liars, for perjurers, and if there is any other thing that is contrary to sound doctrine, [11] according to the glorious gospel of the blessed God which was committed to my trust.

The law is for lawbreakers. If family and civil government agree with the law and justice of God, it reinforces to those under their jurisdiction that they do in fact stand guilty before God when they transgress His law and Word; that they are condemned and in need of redemption. If family government or civil government corrupt their rule, however, and begin to teach things *contrary* to God's law and justice, they have an adverse affect upon those under their jurisdiction. They distort the law and justice of God when they declare good to be evil and evil to be good. Thus, they make it harder for those under their jurisdiction to be instructed in seeing their guilt before God.

The point is that good law which affirms or mirrors the law and justice of God helps men to see their need for Christ. Bad law that contravenes and spurns the law and justice of God assists men in ignoring and/or justifying their sin. Hence, the laws of a nation go to the very salvation of men's souls.

Now Pietism[139] – which teaches that Christianity should be a purely private matter and that God's law has no place in the governance of nations - always tells us that we are wasting our time when it comes to being involved in seeing that good laws are established in our nation. They mock it as mere "moralizing." They say we should just be involved in trying to save men's souls – we should just preach the gospel. But what Pietism fails to understand is that good law – that which mirrors the law

139 Pietism was funded and promoted by government authorities including Frederick in Prussia during the 18th century in order to remove Christianity from the public square and relegate it a mere private matter. To learn more about Pietism, read the following three articles. Matthew Trewhella. *The Destructive Influence of Pietism in American Society*. Mercy Seat Church. Web. < http://www.mercyseat.net/destructivepietism.html> And, *A Brief History of Pietism and Statist Rulers*. Web. <http://www.mercyseat.net/pietismgovart.html> And, Richard V. Pierard, *Why Did Protestants Welcome Hitler? Fides et Historia* 10/2 (Spring 1978): 8–29. Also listen to the sermon, *God DOESN'T Just Expect Sinners to Act Like Sinners* < http://www.mercyseat.net/sermon-audio.html>

and justice of God - helps men see where they are wrong, where they have sinned against God, where they do need to repent.

This is not an either/or dilemma. The Church should call men to repentance and tell people about Jesus, *and* we should also be involved in talking to the magistrates and people of our nation about the importance of good, just law. It is not an either/or – we should do both. We address both the personal and the public.

Scholar and historian, Steven Ozment, rightly points out that the Protestant reformers understood that "Reform that existed only in pamphlets and sermons, and not also in law and institutions, would remain a private affair, confined to all intents and purposes within the minds of preachers and pamphleteers."[140]

The pastors of Magdeburg spoke of the important role the laws of a nation play in the redemptive process of men in their Magdeburg Confession of 1550. The pastors wrote:

> Just as the Church is an ordinance of God, in which God wants there to be an order of teachers and of learners, so also politics and economy[141] are truly ordinances of God, in which He likewise wants there to be an order of superiors and an order of inferiors who are ruled by laws and precepts that agree with reason and are not at variance with the Word, and obey them, not only because of wrath or fear of the punishment which threatens from their rulers, but also because of conscience, that is, fear of the wrath and judgment of God.
>
> For God has armed these His ordinances and powers with fear of both wrath and punishment, divine and human, and they both hold their respective power. And He has distinguished one power from another in His Word, so that He has attributed to each of them its own object and task, and likewise to each its own method of punishment. And although He does not desire the powers to be mixed up with each other, nonetheless He desires them to help each other in turn, so that in the end they all may agree, and that everything in its own place and way principally may promote the

140 Steven Ozment, *Protestants: The Birth of a Revolution* (New York, NY: Doubleday, 1992) 23.

141 By "politics" the pastors mean the civil sphere. By "economy" they mean not only economic life, but social life more broadly considered, especially the family.

> true knowledge of God and His Glory *and their eternal salvation*, or, when it does not attain this ultimate goal, may at least bring about a secondary sort of well-being, that men may live peacefully, uprightly, *kai ouk akarpoi*[142] in this civil manner of life.[143]

Notice that the pastors speak of three of the four governments God has established – church government, civil government, and family government. The pastors call them "ordinances." "Politics" refers to civil government. "Economy" refers to family government. Notice that they say God "desires them [these three governments or ordinances] to help each other in turn, so that in the end they all may agree, and that everything in its own place and way principally may promote the true knowledge of God and His glory *and their [individuals] eternal salvation.*"

Good law that affirms or mirrors the law and justice of God helps men to see their need for Christ. Bad law that contravenes and spurns the law and justice of God helps men to justify their sin. Again, the laws of a nation can impact the very salvation of men's souls.

Good law is good both for the individual when it comes to their salvation, *and* for the governance and protection of society. Notice the pastors went on to say, "or, when it does not attain this ultimate goal, may at least bring about a secondary sort of well-being, that men may live peacefully, uprightly, *kai ouk akarpoi* in this civil manner of life." The *"ultimate goal"* of the law as expressed through all three of these governments – church, civil, and family – is the salvation of men's souls, instructing men they are sinners in need of Christ. If the "ultimate goal" is not realized in an individual life, however, the law still serves to provide good governance and protection to those within society.

The magistrate's legislative action dramatically impacts those under his jurisdiction – whether for good or for bad – and impacts men, both temporally and eternally.

For example, before abortion was legalized in America, babies were still aborted (just as, though we currently have laws against burglary, homes are still broken into). But after abortion was decriminalized, the number of abortions in this nation rose exponentially. Because the

142 not unfruitful

143 Colvin, *Magdeburg Confession*, 41.

magistrate, who possesses authority from God (and whose authority is recognized by the people) has made law stating it is *okay* to kill one's son or daughter in the womb, many people therefore rationalize *it is okay* to kill their son and daughter in the womb.

Now, if the magistrate was to do right in the sight of God and criminalize the murder of the preborn in accordance with the law and justice of God, there would be two results. First, those involved in abortion would more readily see their guilt before God and therefore more readily see their need for Christ, and second, the preborn would be protected from a brutal, heinous death, and far fewer would die.

This is what I mean when I say that good law is good both for the individual when it comes to their salvation – and it is good for the governance and protection of those within society.

Now, if one tries to help pass laws against abortion, the Pietist immediately objects, saying, "That is an utter waste of time - women are not saved by not having abortions, but by hearing the Gospel. We should just preach the Gospel." Though what the Pietist says sounds "spiritual," in reality their position works against men coming to know Christ (not to mention the proliferation of lawlessness it promotes in society).

First, the law of God should be honored among men, and one way it is honored is that it is reflected in the laws of a nation. Second, the preborn should be protected from murder and an unjust death. And third, people who are involved in abortion are more apt to see their guilt (and therefore their need for Christ) if the laws of the nation *do* reflect the law and justice of God.

These truths do not contradict what the Pietist is trying to accomplish – seeing men won to Christ. The two positions are not opposed to each other. It is actually the hope of both positions. The Pietist simply misunderstands that his position actually hinders precisely what he hopes to accomplish.

It is important to understand that the Gospel is never heard in isolation. It is always heard against the background of the cultural milieu in which one lives. If one lives in a culture or nation where good laws prevail that mirror the law and justice of God, one can more readily understand the claims of the Gospel than in a culture or nation where the laws contradict the law and justice of God.

Another prime example of this is homosexuality. Prior to the decriminalization of homosexuality, people more readily recognized it as wrong and evil. Homosexuals would hide their behavior for it was criminal and shameful. Now even Bible-believing churches and Christians (especially younger Christians) question whether it is really a sin. They clearly do not see it for the abhorrent thing God condemns it as in His law and Word.

So then, what the magistrate legislates dramatically impacts those under his jurisdiction – whether for good or for bad.

If the laws of our nation criminalized sodomy, there would be far fewer people involved in it (just as far fewer babies would die if abortion were re-criminalized). Those who did get involved in these defining issues of our day would more readily see their guilt before God and their need for Christ.

We need to remember that the governing authorities are "God's ministers."[144] The authority they possess was delegated to them from God.[145] Their rule is not autonomous. They are to govern according to His rule.

The law and justice of the magistrate are to mirror the law and justice of God. This can affect the very salvation of men's souls. When the law and justice of the magistrate mirror the law and justice of God, men are able to more readily see God's justice and their guilt before Him for violating His law (just as a parent with a child in family government). When the magistrates rebel and make law contrary to God's law, it hinders people from clearly seeing their sin and guilt, and hence, their need for Christ.

> *"When law and morality contradict each other, the citizen has the cruel alternative of either losing his moral sense or losing respect for the law."*[146]
>
> *-Frederic Bastiat, The Law, 1847*

144 Romans 13:4; 2 Chronicles 19:1-7

145 Romans 13:1

146 Frederic Bastiat, *The Law*, (Hudson, NY: Foundation for Economic Education, 1847/2007) 7.

# Appendix C

# The Police Officer as Lesser Magistrate

In January of 1989, Chet Gallagher, a police officer in Las Vegas, Nevada, arrived at an abortion clinic located on Rancho Drive. The place was surrounded by people who had gathered to interpose and blockade the doorway of the deathcamp in an attempt to prevent the killing of preborn babies.

Instead of proceeding to arrest these individuals for their "act of lawlessness" as the other officers were busy doing; Gallagher parked his police motorcycle and in full uniform *joined those blockading the doors.*

This police officer understood his role and duty as a lesser magistrate, as evidenced by the following statement which he read to his fellow officers, and the press recorded:

> I have the sworn responsibility to protect human life. It alone is the highest call and most important duty of every commissioned peace officer. The protecting of human life is the priority that must be considered over less significant property and personal rights of others. Therefore I exercise my discretion as a commissioned law enforcement officer, choosing not to arrest these rescuers, but standing with them in their attempt to prevent certain death to unborn children.

The pastors of Magdeburg referred to "the lowest of the lowest magistrates" using "whatever power they have" to curb tyranny.[147] Police officers could be considered among the lowest level of magistrates in American society.

The police officer does wield power when it comes to either curbing tyranny or carrying it out for superiors. A good police officer can bring justice and protection to a citizenry, while a bad officer can bring injustice and a reign of terror to a citizenry, especially when unjust civil authority rules.

The police officer needs to know that he has a duty *not* to follow orders mindlessly. If an unjust, unconstitutional, or immoral order is given to him by his superior, he has a duty to refuse obedience to that order.

Police officers have a huge impact even upon our freedom to preach the gospel, demonstrate, or protest. Having preached the gospel open-air hundreds of times, and having conducted demonstrations or protests on behalf of the preborn hundreds of times, I have experienced firsthand the difference between a good officer and a bad officer. Our freedom to speak can be greatly curtailed by an officer who just doesn't like our message or just doesn't want us there.

This is not something new. Christians have found themselves at odds with the authorities since the beginning of Christianity. In the book of Acts, the apostles were arrested from time to time by officers of some sort and taken into custody. Church history has innumerable stories of run-ins with the civil authorities, including countless stories about officers themselves, the lowest of magistrates, either helping or harming the Christians.

John Wesley, who preached the gospel open-air for fifty years throughout England and beyond, had many encounters with magistrates or officers, both good and bad. Wesley recalled in his journal an incident where a large group of antagonists against his preaching had gathered causing trouble. In this example, he wrote about the good magistrate:

> The mayor sent order that they [the antagonists] should disperse. But they set him at naught. The chief constable came next in person, who was, till then, sufficiently prejudiced

147 Colvin, *Magdeburg Confession,* 60.

> against us. But they insulted him also in so gross a manner as I believe fully opened his eyes. At length the mayor sent several of his officers who took the ringleaders into custody and did not go till all the rest were dispersed. Surely he hath been to us "the minister of God for good."[148]

In another place, however, he recounted how the officers chased him off in an attempt to prevent him from preaching the gospel. He wrote that a man said to him:

> "Come down; you have no business there." I afterward understood that he was the Mayor of Grampound. Soon after, two constables came and said, "Sir, the mayor says you shall not preach within his borough." I answered, "The mayor has no authority to hinder me. But it is a point not worth contesting." So I went about a musket-shot farther and left the borough to Mr. Mayor's disposal.[149]

Wesley also talked about how he and the Methodists were at times left to the hands of mobs because the officers did not like them. He wrote:

> They broke their [the Methodists] windows, not leaving one whole pane with glass, spoiled their goods, and assaulted their persons with dirt, rotten eggs, and stones whenever they appeared in the street. But no magistrate, though they applied to several, would show them either mercy or justice.[150]

Wesley also recorded an all-points decree that went out in Staffordshire against him and his fellow preachers. The order stated:

> To all High Constables, Petty Constables, and other of his Majesty's Peace Officers: These are, in his Majesty's name, to command you and every one of you, within your respective districts, to make diligent search after the said Methodist

148 John Wesley, *The Journal of John Wesley*, edit. Percy Livingstone Parker (Chicago, IL: Moody Press) 86.

149 Wesley, *Journal*, 224.

150 Wesley, *Journal*, 288.

> preachers, and to bring him or them before some of us his said Majesty's Justices of the Peace, to be examined concerning their unlawful doings. Given under our hands and seals, this October 1743.[151]

Police officers wield discretion that impacts the citizens for good or for bad.

History is full of great stories where an officer of some sort does good to someone being mistreated by the authorities. History is also full of great stories where police officers refuse to obey unjust orders, like Officer Gallagher did at the Las Vegas abortion clinic. Another such officer is Steven Armbruster. He refused to obey an unjust, unconstitutional order by his superior.

On April 18, 2007, approximately 15 members of a Christian group peacefully shared their faith on the campus of Kutztown University in Pennsylvania, including speaking about moral issues such as abortion and homosexual behavior.

Unbeknownst to the Christian group, it was the exact same day Kutztown University had decided to observe the pro-homosexual "Day of Silence." When the crowd caught sight of the Christian group, all homosexual silence went out the window as about 300 protestors from several organizations and clubs descended upon the Christians, loudly opposing their message, and demanding they be thrown off campus.

The university president and the campus police chief, William Mioski, decided to order the Christians off campus, even though it was a public university. Mioskie rallied his men, including officer Steven Armbruster.

The campus police immediately arrested one of the Christians. Mioskie then ordered his officers to "push" the others in the group off campus for "disorderly conduct."

Officer Armbruster understood that this would involve arresting or threatening to arrest the rest of the group, though he saw no evidence of disorderly conduct among the members of the Christian group.

When Armbruster explained to Police Chief Mioskie that he believed such action was unconstitutional and would violate the group's civil

151 Wesley, *Journal,* 126.

rights, Mioskie immediately relieved Armbruster of his duties and told him to leave the scene while other officers executed his orders.

Ultimately, a court dismissed the charges against members of the Christian group who were arrested.

Unfortunately for Officer Armbruster, he was suspended without pay for five working days and warned that he could be fired from his job if he refused to obey an order in the future, *even if the order was unlawful.*

Police officers are not to be mere *machines* for the State. They are human beings. They are to have a conscience. When the State makes immoral or unjust law or a superior gives an unjust or immoral order, they have no obligation to obey; rather they have a duty to resist.

As one former sheriff wrote:

> When we raise our right arm and promise to protect and defend the Constitution, does that oath mean only as far as my supervisor or the Supreme Court allows me to? Or does the oath essentially bestow a responsibility on me to know it, study it, cherish it and ultimately defend it even against a well-meaning but misdirected supervisor or judge? I do not pretend to have all the answers, but I do know the notion that cops should enforce all laws regardless of how abusive, immoral, or unconstitutional they are, is dangerous and destructive.[152]

One organization which teaches men in law enforcement and the military about their duty to *not* obey unjust, unconstitutional, or immoral laws or orders is Oathkeepers.[153] Members agree to a list of ten orders they will not obey, if ever given such an order by a superior.

These are men who understand their function and duty, and refuse to be mere machines for the State.

---

152 Richard Mack, *The Proper Role of Law Enforcement* (1999) 9.

153 Oathkeepers.org

# APPENDIX D

# THE INTERPOSITION OF THE MILITARY:

## SODOMY, A ROGUE CONGRESS, AND THE RULE OF LAW

> *"It is time for you to act O Lord, for they have regarded your law as void."*
>
> *Psalm 119:126*

Just like the lower magistrate must refuse to obey unjust or immoral law by a superior in the civil realm, so are subordinates duty-bound to disobey unjust or immoral orders by superiors in the realm of the military. This has long been established as proper military action.

In First Samuel chapter 22, King Saul ordered his soldiers to kill the priests of the Lord at Nob. He accused the priests of treason, but had no evidence of it except for the testimony of one man, an Edomite named Doeg. The soldiers refused to follow the unjust order by their commander-in-chief. The Scripture reads:

> Then the king said to the guards who stood about him, "Turn and kill the priests of the Lord, because their hand also is with

> David, and because they knew when he fled and did not tell it to me." *But the servants of the king would not lift their hands to strike the priests of the Lord.*[154]

That those in the military have a duty to refuse immoral or unjust commands by their superiors has long been established within American military jurisprudence. The Andersonville Trial of 1865 made it resoundingly clear that a subordinate officer could not use "I was just following the orders of my superiors" as a defense for his participation in carrying out an immoral or unjust command.

The Nuremberg Trials of 1945-1946 made this standard clear to all the world.

In late December of 1989, General Vasile Milea, who was the Romanian Minister of Defense, was ordered by Romania's leader, Nicolae Ceausescu, to shoot demonstrators who opposed Ceausescu's rule. The Romanian Revolution had commenced just a week earlier when secret police attempted to arrest Pastor Laszlo Tokes at his church, and congregants blocked access to the pastor. Others soon joined the church members in this act of interposition which led to a nation-wide rebellion against the tyrant.

General Milea *refused* to obey Ceausescu's order to shoot the demonstrators.

We could use a few men like Vasile Milea among America's military generals today. On Saturday, December 18, 2010, the U.S. Congress passed a law to homosexualize America's military – a blatant attempt to further shove the filth of homosexual behavior upon Americans. The military would be right and just to *disobey* this immoral edict in the days to come.

American military men have both a right and a duty to defy this immoral edict made by Congress and signed into law by their commander-in-chief. That America's military men who disobey are just in their actions is sure. Just consider the situation at hand.

Our nation's Commander-in-Chief, Barack Obama, said upon passage of repealing "Don't Ask, Don't Tell" that allowing open sodomy would make the military "more professional." Pray tell, how does allowing one man to stick his penis into the rectum of another man make the

154 First Samuel 22:17

military "more professional?" That's as absurd as Planned Parenthood always saying they're *"for"* the family while they *kill* family members.

This edict will only demoralize and further effeminize our troops. This is an act that an enemy power would enlist to subvert their foe, and make it more vulnerable.

Yet, to date, no Vasile Milea has appeared. Not one American general has refused to comply with Congress and the President and stand in defiance of this immoral law and the orders that have followed. Already the military is conducting Gay Pride events to indoctrinate young men into accepting homosexuality.[155]

Even the Marines have released to the public some of their indoctrination training. Their materials state that: All troops are expected to shower with homosexuals and sleep in the same barracks. If a Marine spots two men kissing off duty at a shopping mall, he should react as if he is seeing a man and a woman kissing. Marines should accept fellow Marines marching in Gay Pride or Veteran's parades as an expression of free speech. Any Marine recruiters opposed to the new policy cannot refuse a promising applicant because they are homosexual, and might be re-assigned or discharged if they do so.[156]

With each day that passes, the chance of undoing what they have done becomes more difficult. The corrupting influence runs deeper as each military leader and each soldier complies. Meanwhile, the people tolerate this corruption of their military because their consciences have been compromised by the immorality they have accepted and accommodated in their own lives.

The military has a long and prestigious practice in the history of mankind for being the one part of government that acts in an attempt to restore order when the civil magistrates impose immoral and unjust laws. The homosexualization of America's military will weaken their ability to interpose against the unjust and immoral decrees of the Federal government in the future.

---

155 *Military Holds First Event Marking Gay Pride Month.* San Francisco Chronicle. 26 Jun. 2012. Web. <http://www.sfgate.com/politics/article/Military-holds-1st-event-marking-gay-pride-month-3665411.php> Also: Army Sgt. 1st Class Tyrone C. Marshall Jr. *Defense Department Hosts First LGBT Pride Month Event.* U.S. Department of Defense. 26 Jun. 2012. Web. <http://www.defense.gov/News/NewsArticle.aspx?ID=116908>

156 Elliot Spagat. *Marines Get Trained on Accepting Gay Recruits.* Orange County Register. 28 Apr. 2011. Web. <http://www.ocregister.com/articles/marines-298366-pendleton-accepting.html>

If a military man ever does refuse to comply with Congress and the President and stands in defiance of this immoral law, he will be attacked by our government and commander-in-chief as readily as Vasile Milea was by the tyrant Ceausescu. Therefore, it is important that we rally behind such a man because what he is doing is right and just.

When the mantra is thrown up (as it always is) "we must obey the rule of law," we must repudiate such a declaration for the nonsense that it is. The rule of law for nearly 1500 years in Western Civilization was God's law. Over the last 100 years, rebellious men have undermined this fact. There is now no objective standard for the rule of law as God's law has been discarded. Hence, the State now thinks it gets to make up law all by itself, and make it whatever they wish. And as one can detect, things are not going well.

The British jurist, William Blackstone, whose commentary on law shaped American jurisprudence and who was the second most quoted scholar by America's founders, declared of God's laws that *"No human laws should be suffered to contradict these."* Sodomy is a crime under God's law, and so sodomy was outlawed throughout all of Western Civilization.

If any general (or underling) stands in defiance of this current immoral decree by our Congress, those of us who love the only and true rule of law need to support his efforts.

If Congress and the President continue to walk down this dark road of rebellion and anarchy, the military may someday have to rise up and interpose, as they have a long and prestigious history of doing. They may have to declare to our civil magistrates what Roman General Pompey stated to the magistrates of Messana – *"Stop quoting laws to us, we carry swords."*

## Appendix E

# A Biblical Response to Those Who Say We Should Disarm; to Those Who Teach Pacifism; to Those Who Think the Bible Has Nothing to Say About Arms

**Genesis 4:8-12:** In this passage, Scripture records the first murder wherein Cain killed Abel. That Cain must have used some sort of weapon to kill Abel is evidenced by the fact that Abel was bleeding (he was not strangled). Notice how God responded to the killing. He did not institute some sort of weapon-control, rather, He punished the one who committed the crime.

**Exodus 20 and following:** In God's holy law, which He decreed at Sinai, nowhere do you see God outlawing weapons in response to the various crimes which He prohibited in His legislation. He always punishes the perpetrator. He never disarms the citizenry.

**Exodus 22:2:** In this verse, God declares that if someone breaks into your house at night and you kill him, you are not guilty of murder. This verse makes clear that you have a God-given right to defend yourself and to defend your family.

**Deuteronomy 22:23-27:** This passage deals with rape. Notice that verse 27 ends with the words "but there was no one to save her." What is the implication of such a statement? The implication is that had someone been around to hear her cry out, they had a moral duty to intervene and protect her from being raped. To stand by would be immoral. We have a God-given right to defend not only ourselves, but also others.

**Numbers 1:** In God's economy, He instituted an armed citizenry, not a standing army, in order to deal with the affairs of war regarding Israel. This is what the Founding Fathers of America envisioned for our nation. Even in Switzerland today, every home is furnished with a machine gun (one of the reasons Hitler chose not to invade Switzerland).

**I Samuel 13:19-22:** The Philistines disarmed the Israelites. Weapon-control was instituted. No blacksmiths were allowed lest the Israelites arm themselves. A disarmed people is the sign of a conquered people. A disarmed people is the sign of an enslaved people.

**Isaiah 2:1-5:** Many, including the United Nations, take the latter part of verse 4 in this passage, which states "they shall beat their swords into plowshares, and their spears into pruning hooks," and try to say that God wants us to disarm. The context makes clear, however, that "swords will be beaten into plowshares and spears into pruning hooks" when God rules, not when the United Nations or any other government of man rules.

**Matthew 5:38-39:** In this passage, Jesus is not denigrating the law of God in regards to one's right to defend himself and others, rather He is repudiating the *lex talionis* - the law of retaliation, which said, "if someone messes you up today, you go back and mess him up five times worse tomorrow." The Pharisees were even using the law of God to justify this mindset. Jesus is repudiating this personal vengeance which some sought to justify and participate in. He is not saying we cannot defend ourselves or others.

Vengeance belongs to God (Romans 12:19; Deuteronomy 32:35; Proverbs 20:22). We are not to avenge ourselves. If we see someone who needs our help during the commission of a crime, we have a God-given right and duty to intervene. If, however, the crime has been committed (past tense), we have no God-given right or duty to go and execute judgment upon the perpetrator. God will avenge. God will judge.

God has given the sword (a symbol of judgment) to the civil magistrate (Romans 13:4). If a crime has been committed, it is to be reported to the civil authorities and they have a God-given right and duty before God to execute judgment.

**Matthew 26:51-52:** Some try to say that this passage proves that Jesus was a pacifist and against guns. Quite the contrary. Where does Jesus tell Peter to put his sword? "In its place." John makes it clearer: Jesus said to Peter "Put your sword into the sheath" (John 18:11). Jesus didn't tell him to melt it down into a plowshare, rather he told him to put it "into the sheath." The sword has its proper place. It is not evil. But Peter wanted to use it in an improper situation. Jesus came to earth to die. Peter would be abrogating the purposes of God if he intervened with the sword. As Jesus goes on to say in verse 11 of John chapter 18, "Shall I not drink the cup which My Father has given Me?" Jesus was trying to teach His disciples that His Kingdom is not expanded in the earth through the use of force, rather it is expanded through the preaching of the Gospel and the discipling of the nations.

If someone wants to live by the sword, they will die by the sword, as Jesus says. In other words, he who uses the sword for improper purposes will die by it. It was improper for Peter to have used it in that situation. A criminal or a tyrant who uses the sword improperly will rightly die by it. But the use of the sword in a proper fashion, to defend one's person or one's family or one's country, is not condemned by Scripture, rather Scripture upholds it.

God is not a pacifist. Jesus is not a pacifist. As Jesus said in the very next verse, verse 53, "Or do you think that I cannot now pray to My Father, and He will provide Me with more than twelve legions of angels?" Jesus could have used force. The use of force; the use of swords was simply improper for the situation in which Christ was involved. He was supposed to die. He and the Father are not pacifists. He did not use force because He had to drink the cup of the Father.

**Exodus 15:3:** This verse of Scripture declares the Lord to be a "man of war." That God is not a pacifist is evidenced throughout Scripture. Even Jesus Himself, who is the brightness of God's glory and the express image of His person, and who has declared all that God is (Hebrews 1:3; John 1:18), drove the moneychangers out of the temple with a whip and overturned their tables (John 2:15). The book of Revelation defines Him as a King who does what? "Judges and makes war" (Revelation 19:11). The Scripture declares that Jesus Christ is "the same yesterday, today, and forever" (Hebrews 13:8). God's character does not change. God is not a pacifist.

In closing, there are some who say that "we should not have guns; we should just trust God." My response to those who say this is - "Let me ask you, do you have a lock on your front door?" They always say "yes." I then ask, "Do you lock it when you leave or go to bed at night?" Those who live in the city always say "yes." I then ask, "Why do you have a lock on your door? Why don't you just trust God?"

Just because we have a lock on our door or a gun in our closet does not mean we are trusting in them to protect us with the same trust with which we're to trust the Lord.

Rather, we simply see the wisdom and prudence of having such things in order to be good stewards in protecting our belongings and our families.

The psalmist understood that there was no contradiction. David said in verse one of Psalm 144: "Blessed be the Lord my Rock, who trains my hands for war, and my fingers for battle." He then said in verse two: "My lovingkindness and my fortress, my high tower and my deliverer, my shield and the one in whom I take refuge."

# A SUMMARY OF THE DOCTRINE OF THE LESSER MAGISTRATES

## The Doctrine of the Lesser Magistrates

The lesser magistrate doctrine declares that when the superior or higher civil authority makes unjust/immoral laws or decrees, the lesser or lower ranking civil authority has both a right and duty to refuse obedience to that superior authority. If necessary, the lesser authorities even have the right and obligation to actively resist the superior authority.

## Rooted in Interposition:

*Interposition* is that calling of God which causes one to step into the gap-willingly placing oneself between the oppressor and his intended victim. Interposition takes place when someone or some group interposes or positions themselves between an oppressor and the intended victim.

When it comes to the interposition of the lesser magistrate, he interposes for the people – placing himself between the unjust laws or decrees of the higher authority and the people. He also acts in defense of the rule of law. The interposition of the lesser magistrates abates the just judgment of God on nations that have impugned His law.

## All Authority is Delegated:

The lesser magistrate doctrine reminds the higher authority that their authority is limited. No one who holds authority in civil government rules with autonomy. The authority they possess is delegated to them by God. Hence, all those in positions of authority stand accountable to God, and are to govern according to His rule.

A tyrant is defined as one who contravenes or impugns the law of God; assaults the person, property, or liberty of the citizens; or violates the Constitution.

### Primary Duty of Lesser Magistrates is Threefold:

First, they are to oppose and resist any laws or edicts from the higher authority that contravene the law or Word of God. Second, they are to protect the person, liberty, and property of those who reside within their jurisdiction from any unjust or immoral actions by the higher authority. Third, they are not to implement any laws or decrees made by the higher authority that violate the Constitution, and if necessary, resist them.

### God's Law is the Objective Standard:

The law of God is that objective standard so that men know when governments are making unjust or immoral law. The disobedience of the lesser magistrate is not subjective. He is only justified in defying the higher authority when the higher authority clearly contravenes the law of God, or makes law which is clearly an attack upon the person, liberty, or property of the people in the lesser magistrate's jurisdiction, or makes law or policy which violates the Constitution.

### The Rule of Law:

The rule of law simply stated is: *the law is king*. All are subject to the laws of the land, both king and commoner, both government officials and citizens, and that law is equitable to all. They formalized God's moral law, along with biblical principles of authority and government, under what became known as "the rule of law." This became known as the rule of law in Western Civilization for nearly 1500 years.

The rule of law is crumbling. As America collapses because it has spurned the law of God as the rule of law, we will be presented with an opportunity when godly lesser magistrates will need to stand in the gap. They will need to interpose for the sake of the rule of law, for the sake of the people they represent, and defy bad law. They will be accused by the tyrant higher authority of anarchy and destroying the rule of law, but in reality, they are the ones defending it.

## The Pastors of Magdeburg:

The doctrine of the lesser magistrates was first formalized in the *Magdeburg Confession* by the Lutheran pastors in Magdeburg, Germany in 1550. Other Reformers built upon the doctrine.

## John Knox:

The best treatise ever written on the doctrine of the lesser magistrates was by John Knox in his *Appellation to the Nobility and Estates of Scotland (1558)*. Knox made clear that lesser magistrates are not to hide behind the excuse that they must simply obey those in authority above them. Knox stated disdainfully, "For now the common song of all men is, 'We must obey our kings, be they good or be they bad; for God has so commanded.'"

Christopher Goodman's *How Superior Powers Ought to be Obeyed by Their Subjects and Wherein They May Lawfully by God's Word be Disobeyed and Resisted (1558)* is also an excellent work.

## Rogue Lesser Magistrates:

Lesser magistrates, just like superior magistrates, can act unjustly. When they do, it is the duty of the higher magistrate, equal fellow magistrates, or even a subordinate to the unjust magistrate, to interpose and rein in that lesser magistrate. When tyranny presents itself, almost never do all the lesser magistrates stand and resist, whether the oppression and tyranny comes from the higher magistrate or from other lesser magistrates. Even when some lesser magistrates take a stand, usually the majority will go along with the tyranny.

## The Tyrannical Higher Magistrate:

The higher authority likes to be obeyed. The lesser magistrates and the people must understand that when they interpose against unjust law, there will be a fight. Their reputation will be maligned, and they could end up imprisoned or abused in some fashion by the higher authority. A governing official needs to understand that they act *not* for glory or political ambition - rather they do so because it is the right thing to do in the sight of God.

## The Role of the People:

The role of the people in applying the lesser magistrate doctrine is to remonstrate before the lesser magistrate, and rally behind him when he takes a stand. The lesser magistrates often will not act until the people plead their case, and the magistrates are assured of their support.

## The Future:

When will the lesser magistrates stand in defiance of Federal tyranny? The question that remains to be seen in the events of our day is – will the lesser magistrates merely squabble with the Federal government or higher authority over matters of dispute, *or will they stand resolute in opposition to their abuse of power*? Lesser magistrates today need to understand that state governments were not intended to be mere conduits for enacting Federal public policies. They are not to be mere implementation centers through which the Federal government dispenses its unjust policies, decisions, and laws. The interposition of the lesser magistrates is absolutely critical for the preservation of liberty. The hour for them to stand is upon us.

# PARTIAL BIBLIOGRAPHY


Abels, Richard. *Alfred the Great: War, Culture and Kingship in Anglo-Saxon England.* New York: Longman, 1998.

Baker, Hunter. *The End of Secularism.* Wheaton: Crossway, 2009.

Baldwin, Timothy, and Baldwin, Chuck. *Romans 13: The True Meaning of Submission.* Xlibris, 2011.

Bartley, David D. *John Witherspoon and the Right of Resistance.* Ph.D. dissertation, Ball State University, 1989.

Bastiat, Frederic. *The Law.* Auburn: Tribeca Books (mises.org), 1847/2007.

Beik, William. *Urban protest in seventeenth-century France.* Cambridge: Cambridge University Press, 1997.

Beza, Theodore. *On the Right of Magistrates - 1574.* trans. Henry-Louis Gonin, ed. Patrick S. Poole. <http://www.constitution.org/cmt/beza/magistrates.htm>

Black, Henry Campbell. *Black's Law Dictionary.* St. Paul: West Publishing Co., 1978.

Blackstone, William. *Commentaries on the Laws of England* Vol.1 Philadelphia: Childs & Peterson, 1765/1860.

Brutus, Stephanus Junius. *Vindiciae, Contra Tyrannos (or, concerning the legitimate power of a prince over the people, and of the people over a prince).* ed. & trans. George Garnett. Cambridge: Cambridge University Press, 1994.

Clavier, Henri. *The Duty and The Right of Resistance (according to the Bible and to the Church).* Oxford: Blackwell, 1956.

Codevilla, Angelo M. *The Character of Nations.* New York: Basic Books, 2009.

Danzinger, Danny, and John Gillingham. *1215: The Year of Magna Carta.* New York: Touchstone, 2004.

Demar, Gary. *God and Government Vol.1-3.* Brentwood: Wolgemuth & Hyatt Publishers, 1989.

Dorchester, Daniel. *Christianity in the United States.* Powder Springs: American Vision Press, 1888/2009.

Eberle, Christopher J. *Religious Convictions in Liberal Politics.* Cambridge: Cambridge University Press, 2002.

Goodman, Christopher. *How Superior Powers Ought to be Obeyed by Their Subjects and Wherein They May Lawfully by God's Word be Disobeyed and Resisted (1558).* Kessinger Publishing, Kessinger.net.

Greaves, Richard L. *Glimpses of Glory: John Bunyan and English Dissent.* Stanford: Stanford University Press, 2002.

Halbrook, Stephen P. *That Every Man Be Armed.* Oakland: Independent Institute, 1984.

Headley, Joel T. *The Forgotten Heroes of Liberty.* Birmingham: Solid Ground Christian Books, 1861/2005.

Hoadly, Benjamin. *The measures of submission to the civil magistrate considered.* London: ECCO Print Editions, 1718/2010.

Hogue, Arthur R. *Origins of the Common Law*. Indianapolis: Liberty Press, 1966/1985.

Hotman, Francois, and Theodore Beza, and Philippe Mornay. *Constitutionalism and Resistance in the Sixteenth Century (Three Treatises by Hotman, Beza, and Mornay)*. tran. & ed. Julian H. Franklin. New York: Pegasus, 1969.

Houghton, S.M. *Sketches from Church History*. Carlisle: Banner of Truth Trust, 1980.

Hume, David. *The History of England*. New York: Harper & Brothers Publishers, 1688/1851.

John of Salisbury, *The Statesman's Book of John of Salisbury – Policraticus*. trans. John Dickinson. New York: Russell & Russell, 1159/1963.

Jones, E. Michael. *Libido Dominandi: Sexual Liberation and Political Control*. South Bend: St. Augustine's Press, 2000.

Josephus, Flavius. *The Works of Flavius Josephus*. trans. William Whiston. Philadelphia: Jas. B. Smith & Co., 94/1854.

Justinian. *Justinian's Institutes*. tran. Peter Birks & Grant Mcleod. Ithaca: Cornell University Press, 1987.

Kelly, Douglas F. *The Emergence of Liberty in the Modern World*. Phillipsburg: P&R Publishing, 1992.

Kettering, Sharon. *Judicial politics and urban revolt in seventeenth-century France: The Parlement of Aix, 1629-1659*. Princeton: Princeton University Press, 1978.

Knox, John. *Selected Writings of John Knox*. edit. Kevin Reed. Dallas: Presbyterian Heritage Publishing, 1557/1995.

Knox, John. *History of the Reformation in Scotland*. edit. William Dickinson, Vol.2. New York: Philosophical Library, 1558/1950.

Kostlin, Julius. *The Life of Martin Luther.* Edit. John G. Morris. Philadelphia: Lutheran Publication Society, 1883.

Kurtz, Professor. *Church History.* trans. Rev. John Macpherson, Vol.1-3. New York: Funk & Wagnalls Company, 1888.

Lewis, C.S. *God in the Dock.* Grand Rapids: Eerdmans Publishing Company, 1970.

Mayhew, Jonathan. *A Discourse Regarding Unlimited Submission and Non-Resistance to the Higher Powers.* Northridge: Santa Susana Press, 1750/1976.

Olson, Oliver. *Theology of Revolution: Magdeburg 1550-1551. Sixteenth Century Journal* 3, no.1 (1972).

Ozment, Steven. *Protestants: The Birth of a Revolution.* New York: Doubleday, 1992.

Palmer, Robert C. *Liberty and Community: Constitution and Rights in the Early American Republic.* New York: Oceana, 1987.

Parker, T.M. *Christianity and the State in the Light of History.* London: Black 1955.

Ponet, John. *A Short Treatise on Political Power, and of the true obedience which subjects owe to kings and other civil governors, with an Exhortation to all true and natural English men (1556).* trans. Patrick S. Poole. Web. < http://www.constitution.org/cmt/ponet/polpower.htm>

Rein, Nathan. *The Chancery of God: Protestant Print, Polemic and Propaganda against the Empire, Magdeburg 1546 -1551.* Burlington: Ashgate, 2008.

Rushdoony, Rousas John. *Christianity and the State.* Vallecito: Ross House Books, 1986.

Rutherford, Samuel. *Lex Rex (or, The Law and The Prince)*. Harrisonburg: Sprinkle Publications, 1644/1982.

Schaeffer, Francis. *A Christian Manifesto. Westchester: Crossway Books, 1981.*

Schlossberg, Herbert. *Idols for Destruction: Christian Faith and Its Confrontation with American Society.* Nashville: Thomas Nelson Publishers, 1983.

Skinner, Quentin. *The Foundations of Modern Political Thought.* Cambridge: Cambridge University Press, 1978.

Smith, Preserved. *The Age of the Reformation. New York: Henry Holt and Company, 1920.*

Smith, Steven D. *Foreordained Failure: The Quest for a Constitutional Principle of Religious Freedom.* New York: Oxford University Press, 1995.

Tokes, Laszlo. *The Fall of Tyrants*. Wheaton: Crossway Books, 1990.

Von Humboldt, Wilhelm. *The Limits of State Action*. edit. J.W. Burrow. Indianapolis: Liberty Fund, 1792/1993.

Wilson, James. *The Works of James Wilso*n, Vol.1, edit. James Dewitt Andrews. Chicago: Callaghan and Company, 1792/1896.

Witte Jr., John. *The Reformation of Rights: Law, Religion, and Human Rights in Early Modern Calvinism*. New York: Cambridge University Press, 2007.

Whitford, David Mark. *Tyranny and Resistance: The Magdeburg Confession and the Lutheran Tradition*. St. Louis: Concordia Publishing House, 2001.

Zimmerman, Carle C. *Family and Civilization*. Wilmington: ISI Books, 1947/2008.

# Further Writings on the Doctrine of the Lesser Magistrates

**The Appellation - 1558**
John Knox
Selected Writings of John Knox
Kevin Reed, editor
Presbyterian Heritage Publishing, 1995

**How Superior Powers Ought to be Obeyed by Their Subjects and Wherein They May Lawfully by God's Word be Disobeyed and Resisted - 1558**
Christopher Goodman
Kessinger.net

**On the Rights of Magistrates - 1574**
Theodore Beza
http://constitution.org/cmt/beza/magistrates.htm

**LesserMagistrate.com**
The author has established this website as a clearinghouse for those interested in this doctrine. You will find up to date news stories and historical articles, as well as other resources. You can contact Matthew Trewhella there, or at MercySeat.net.

Made in the USA
Middletown, DE
11 March 2021